CONTENTS

NEW WAVE
FOR A
MUSICIAN

FOR THOSE WHO EXPECT A CHANGE

AMARANATH RANATUNGA

Amazon.com

New Wave for a Musician

ISBN: 978-624-94737-0-6

Cover design: Amaranath Ranatunga

Published by: Amazon.com

AMARANATH RANATUNGA

3

PREFACE

Every product, service, and concept in the world is constantly changing. It must happen to move forward. Therefore, the playing of musical instruments should also lead to a change. As the thoughts and thoughts of man change with this change due to transformations, he also expects this change in the music he listens to. It is not surprising that people are moving towards new ideas, attitudes, and transformations due to the day's great upheaval and social changes. It must be seen by the player and that understanding must be reflected in his performance. Therefore, there must be a change in the playing and new genres must be born.

In this book, I have analyzed how a player steps towards a change in playing, its plan, how to achieve the change, its value, its method, and approach, and finally how to socialize the new wave in music. Musical instruments used in the world become less popular with time and some musical instruments can be seen leaving the field forever. This book explains the reasons for these transformations and includes an analysis of how an instrument continued to be popular with the new wave throughout its lifetime.

This is not the time to explore the reasons for such failures in this age where certain rules and plans used are proven to fail due to their inadequacy. It's no secret that it doesn't happen that way, either on a stroke of luck or as a reality. Therefore, it is important not only to represent the field of play in your search or continuous involvement in events but also to be in touch with the dynamics of its transformations and even the slightest movements. You can never experience or feel that transformation if you only engage in composing as your mind and action are aligned to it, so it may be difficult for you to experience this transformation. That way you will not see the change that needs to be grasped that appears before you. Your delay will be very acute when you realize that people have not rallied around you after achieving the goals you pursued. During such a prolonged existence, your creativity also becomes monotonous. Therefore, you must maintain both these profiles equally in your journey. It is for the long existence of the player and the field.

There are a few cases where certain things that have been stated have been accurately confirmed. Because it's practical level is a different process than what is stated. Words are easy to use. Similarly, dreaming has happened throughout history. However, it is tragic if the opinion is not with a strong foundation for the musician to overcome the competition.

Therefore, I think that this book will be a foundation for a player who is searching for a new wave.

Amaranath Ranatunga
September 2023

ACKNOWLEDGEMENT

Nothing meaningful can be built all alone. I like to acknowledge and express my gratitude to the following people for their invaluable support and contribution to publishing this book. I would like to honor them.

My dearest friend Shakya Nanayakkara for his valuable contribution and offering many meaningful suggestions and my student Chiran Prabash. Masha Patikirikoral for reviewing the entire writing with meaningful suggestions.

I thank amazon.com for publishing my book as an eBook and Paper Book.

I am eternally grateful to my Guitar. It has been an inspiration in my professional and personal life, and I hope this book will help you to create a new wave in your playing career. Finally, I thank you all.

Amaranath Ranatunga
September 2023

DEDICATION

To my wife Merlyn, daughter Durga and son Aravinda

INTRODUCTION

Players today face a great challenge as some musical instruments and playing styles have reached their climax in producing rhythms tones colors and patterns so the players must invent new styles of playing or new waves to maintain their popularity. Many newcomers to the playing field are at risk if they only imitate and follow a popular player and his genre. The author of this book discusses how to build such a new wave, after analyzing the own potential and opportunities of the player and developing a vision and plan of action for innovation.

- How to face failures, defeats, and maintaining a player's existence throughout the carrier is explained well in the book, and motivating for a long and stable journey is also discussed.
- Describing the changes or transformations that took place from the day music was born to the present is a very complicated task. In ancient times Middle Ages, Renaissance, Baroque, Classical, Romantic and 20th and 21st Century, transformation took place slowly and often took a hundred years or more, but today it is changing very rapidly in a year or a few months.
- The rise of social media is rapidly changing the world's technologies, architecture, fashion, furniture, cars, roads, cities, and many others. In such a world, music only cannot remain unchanged.
- The people facing this change are lining up for a transformation. Therefore, people are expecting a change

in everything, as well as in music.

- The players have reached the end of a long journey with that musical instrument or have not been able to go beyond the playing style of that instrument. Since there are no restrictions on the instruments, the players must use all the possibilities available with those instruments.
- In this book, the procedure, and knowledge that a player should have to establish such a wave, the method that builds his mind for it, the system of using that knowledge and procedure, the methods of socializing a new wave, and the pattern that maintain it continuously and the way of keeping the performer in the field are also thoroughly analyzed.
- An analysis of the role of the player and what level he should be in today's context is a leading theme discussed in this book. The book discusses why this task should be done and how it should be done.

The author discusses and vividly explains the present complexity of the giant music industry and gives ideas to establish successful methods to overcome those unseen problems. In any field, if the competition is high and broad, there is a collapse, and sometimes is not easy to rebuild it properly. The value of more new organizations to promote newcomers enter to the field is a must and their knowledge and the activities for this task are discussed.

September 2023

My guitar is silent
How I sought its deep voice
Not fingers know it
Did my heart tell me
Become the sound
Is there anything lovely there
Is there something deeper
I strive for that
But it is not a surprise
It is real

If not

Why the audience

To my guitar

There was a shout of joy

Amaranath

PLAYER'S INTRODUCTION

Chapter 1

"Your instrument is calm, it's powerful and ready,
It is only your delay".

When defining an instrumentalist, his or her qualities, abilities, and relationships are very important consider. His or her future success depends on such qualities. This has been observed throughout history. Before even identifying the role of an instrumentalist, it is important to see what level he or she should be at present. Many aspects have been changed in history. But in current context where transformations, inventions, usage, constructions, and relationships have changed rapidly, an analysis of an instrumentalist's role and what level he or she should be at present is a main theme discussed in this book. Despite all other changes, today's players need to understand the change in the way of playing and its development. It is time to set foot on this path. Achieving the desired change is your task. This book will create a fruitful discussion about it. It will discuss why this task should be done and how it should be done.

Even though early musicians performed only in royal palaces, today it has flourished, and masses have access to the music created by musicians. These musicians, who have become very popular and turned into millionaires, now play the role of indispensable people pleasing the world. Therefore, nowadays many people in the world are more interested in music and the role of an instrumentalist.

The soloist performs a solo performance and controls every aspect of it. Being a member of a band means sharing responsibility with other members. Therefore, all the responsibilities of the soloist over the performance must be borne by the performer alone. He or she has to offer the audience a message to enjoy and make them satisfied. Therefore, the player is expressing his opinion and communicating the ideas he has gathered based on his experience or a personal idea. According to Western music tradition, it can be described as an art that expresses the ideas or meanings of the player. This performer must have excellent presentation skills. His music is listened to by a group of listeners from different backgrounds and cultures. He must satisfy all these people with a message because he is paid for this task.

It is the player's effort to translate the ideas musically and express them directly, and the musician's existence will be determined by the grasp of the listener's mind and memory. It is a support for the listener's music existence or the future journey of life and will determine the player's popularity and existence. Man is always looking for something new and different for his satisfaction. This is for his knowledge, wisdom or progress. Thus, if what he is looking for or what he expected is included in the player's performance, it will be a great benefit. Hence, the player should try to bring out a meaning, feeling and something new [a message or an idea] through his playing. It is for his survival.

No matter what musical instrument you play, at the end of your performance, there must be a message that can surprise the listener. A player must create memories in the listener's heart. Those memories must be able to satisfy the listener for a long time in his mind. That is why not all players in the field can reach the peak of popularity. The demand for that performer will rise to a higher level of popularity as the listener's sense of wonder increases. There should be a sense of wonder in acting. A novelist's plot must have a sense of wonder. A player's sportsmanship should be awe-inspiring. A singer should have wondered in his singing. If that were not the case, all these people would be ordinary musicians, ordinary players, ordinary novelists, or ordinary singers without recognition. Despite the abundance of the underprivileged population in society, many people in the world remain with a great appetite for the process of making heroes. Therefore, you, who appear as players, are lined up for the task of uplifting such a group of people in society. Therefore, your preparation is very well-timed.

For a player who has mastered his instrument well and knows it well, a path to victory is opened. Ardent practice that leads to its long existence is the second effort. Even if the resources and knowledge are perfected, there must be methods controlled by sharp intelligence to manage it well and popularize it. Competence is mandatory. Without it, there will be no shadow of a solid journey. Any journey without intelligence, to perfect potential, will result in backsliding. A person with intelligence, ability, and good management will conquer every opposition, enemy, and oppressor and win the opportunities without many difficulties. Thus, as soon as one's path becomes strong, one will surely acquire powerful support and recognition from society. For this, it is necessary to learn the right technique, train steadily, and find the right way. For a player to be respected for his performance by those around him, he must have fine playing, confidence, virtue, courage, and discipline along with dedication. A person with these qualities will be aligned with society, no matter what field he represents. Therefore, it is natural that the audience or those who gathered in support of the player should say goodbye at every moment when these qualities are impaired. It is therefore very important for him to be aware of the strong and meaningful message of his creation presented to society. Is it not important for a player to enter a new wave for his survival? Looking at the music from a different perspective beyond the established range is this attempt to socialize a new wave of change. It is best accomplished by changing the perspective and concepts of his music. A group of people who do not have a deep understanding of playing but are very fond of listening will see a profile that was empty until now with this new change of angle. It is illuminated by those new concepts, and they merge with it based on this new interpretation. The player must have a good understanding and appreciation of society and the audience. How many compositions are published in the world per day? [Spotify only publish more than one hundred thousand songs and pieces per day]. There is too much music in the world. Not all of this captured the audience and become popular but only a small part of it touched the hearts of the audience is a good example of this. Only a few creations meet the goals and standards and become perfect. For this reason, it is not appropriate to make an assessment based on the province or the country you live in.

People's thoughts, behaviors, and lifestyles can be changed. It has been happening since the beginning of civilization through various consumer goods and services. For example, who has promoted to wear the pair of shoes you are wearing? Who made a razor mandatory to shave with at the start of the day? Who has inspired to drink a cup of coffee containing the famous coffee grown in Brazil two or three times a day? Some players have realized that such an act is important in the field of music as in all the societies, the dynamics are controlled by someone. Every human being in the world has lined up to stand up for someone.

Just as water has no color or shape, the wind has no proper rhythm or order. This is its nature. But our lives must have shape, color, rhythm, and order. Monitor your heart rate. It has a perfect rhythm. Look at your walking style. It is in good order. Study the position of your body organs. It also has a suitable positioning. Each of these postures or positions is powerful, but some people's existence is very sadly disorientated. The player's presence, proper rhythm, order, harmony and color should stand out more strongly than in other lives. Otherwise, you will appear to have failed to represent the role of the player.

Almost any object you encounter has a shape, a color, a rhythm, and some certain perfection embedded in it. The facts are otherwise you will not get close to that object. When the player lacks these qualities in his playing, he will also be a person without the proper qualities that separate him from others. Music has a strong form, harmony, rhythm, and color. These qualities should be reflected in the life of the player and should be strongly intertwined with his being. Often, we will understand this well when we study the world's greatest musicians. Rarely, do two similar processes often emerge strongly. But it must be so for the strong existence of the player. As soon as the music emerges, even if the music becomes popular, eventually the creator or the performer will be immortalized in the listener's memory. Today, like playing through electronic media such as YouTube or TikTok, the audience gets an opportunity to see the creator or the performer, and through it, the performer or his name is deeply embedded in the hearts of the listeners after such a performance.

Throughout history, man has continued the process of giving something, and today it can be seen to be impaired. Looking at the current human existence, you will realize that words, smiles, and even simple services that can be given without any effort are lost to some degree. If you cannot give something, there will be a problem with your existence. Everyone who can give something so strongly will be labeled as the world strongest. You are the same as a musician. To achieve the strength of the playing, you must highlight a strong aspect of the playing that the listener must embrace thoroughly, and that exchange was the theme of the technique. This attention also highlights the strength of your playing and your presence. In the Feudal system, the exchange of goods took a major place, and the theme of that system was also the exchange. The pattern of this Feudal system is the life of the performer. That is the exchange of something, where an idea, rhythm, harmony or feeling is an investment and then the popularity is expected as a demand or results. You need to think deeply about the message you are trying to convey and have a good understanding of the current pattern of the music industry, the styles it contains, and the musicians that roam around. That study will be very useful for the player before popularizing his creation. Entering the field of music as a musician is one of the greatest challenges. As such, it is strenuous work. Identifying it and examining the music field and its structure should be the starting point for the performer. There is nothing that could be gained by free-flowing behavior in a particular field. Such characters can be seen in any field and whether they live in that field forever or for a short period, they live in a limited dream world and there will be no possibility and opportunity to be a light to society or that field. Such people will not make any progress or influence, and they will not have any advantage or substance to be gained by staying there. Unfortunately, they lack a comprehensive understanding of the subject of contemporary music and an appreciation of its current status. The fact that one's existence is not recognized is well understood when one observes the behavior patterns or daily activities of certain people. However, we will sometimes be surprised by the lack of understanding and interest in these characters. Huge numbers of people who do not utilize the world's resources and opportunities and decide to live as mediocre men are huge. This could be easily seen not only by a player who has laid the foundation for a strong journey but also by a strongman anywhere who strives to achieve strength.

The main reason for the failure of some musicians is that they did not approach this subject correctly at the beginning of their playing career. Facing such problems and failures is inevitable where initiation fails. After this kind of exploration, it becomes clear to you that the number that leads to the strength of the instrument is very limited. Therefore, a path of victory is certain for one who strongly turns to it. What is required is to build firm goals, objectives, and methods and focus on them correctly.

Temporary healing through omissions, postponements, backsliding, and refuse has become a pervasive and invisible problem throughout the world. Even if the intellectual sees this, most people do not see it, and the number of people who are wandering towards failure is increasing day by day, and the time has come for many positive thoughts and modern methods to be presented in a more profound and correct manner. These thoughts must be established in individuals from school age. We rarely get to see a late embrace. But it is some consolation if they embrace this process, even if delayed.

You must be very careful about the correctness of your playing. Stepping onto the stage, you have a great responsibility that cannot be evaded. Not only have you entered a long-term planned practice to fulfill it with discipline to bring it out well, but you must also clearly recognize that strong responsibility of yours to fulfill it. It is natural for humans to make mistakes. Likewise, any language has a very beautiful set of words to deny that fault. But even though the musician's playing contains that beautiful meaning, but the words do not contain any value, if there was any slightest mistake in his performance. What could the player say about the mistake or omission after it is over? The death of the patient is caused by a physician's wrong or delayed administration of drugs or treatment the words are useless for such an omission. A samurai warrior's slightest delay may lead to the end of his life. And then can he say anything about that delay? A car accident happened suddenly. Can he say something and apologize? Those problems cannot be solved or satisfied through words.

There is no need for a discourse on the forgiveness of the world for such mistakes or incidents. But these words which are used by the society for the sake of customs, the man is satisfied to some extent and the player must be aware of the discernment of whether it is meaningful. If you don't have a line-up ready to throw away the forgiveness in the event of a mistake, your willingness to stand out strongly for the correctness of the playing should be aligned strongly without any delay. Apology for any errors in performance is shameful. A strong player should not be in such a frame. His direction should be to become an energetic bold or daring character goes beyond that in playing. Bowing is a rule at the end of the play. It is an ascent to an analysis of your humility. But surrender before a mistake will lead to character assassination. Therefore, the proper player not only becomes a rare character beyond other fields, but it is mandatory to be concerned about building such a personality. Bowing is a display of vigor and duty. Forgiveness is a humiliation of oneself. Apologizing means you win someone's sympathy. A strong performer should be able to gain strength.

In your journey as a musician, you must be careful not only of your playing but also of many flaws and weaknesses in your being. These actions will directly affect the strength you are trying to acquire. The world lacks proper and perfect people. It is a popular opinion that there are only two people, perfect and righteous in the world. One of them died yesterday. The other is not yet born. Although there is no such fair society in the world, in the name of the strength of playing, you must be genuine in your playing from your heart. You should be aware and be careful about it. The most important of these is the way you analyze and interpret others' playing and their standards. So don't be a critic in front of people for a moment. Always be aware of the following four things.

i. Never start an argument or criticism with anyone, about others' performances or their character. Because even if you win that argument, he will hate you forever. Your friendship with him will be damaged. Make sure that others in your field never become estranged or conflict with you. Even if you win the argument, that friend or the person who was involved in that argument will be separated from you forever. No matter what field you stay in, it's sad to see people like this leave you.

ii. If you see the flaws in a certain player's playing, then don't worry about criticizing that with others. It will directly break your dominance and affect your very existence. Don't think of going beyond that unless you see the flaws in their playing and try to correct those weaknesses in yourself. If the strength of the creation or the ability of the player is visible, praising its accuracy and strength will be very important for your existence.

iii. Another's meaningful existence is a lesson to others. See it properly.

iv. As a player you must stay in your field for a long period, and you can stay in this field. Because mental fatigue directly affects brain activity in playing, playing is labeled as a process that uses minimal physical effort, and it is an ideal profession for a long journey. Therefore, try to keep up with other players in your field. If it is not possible, avoid confrontations and arguments with them as much as possible. If you feel any influence from other players, it is very wise to stay away from them quietly. Likewise, it is a great investment for your survival.

The world is full of criticism for the sake of criticism. You listen to them. But be careful to discuss the weaknesses in your playing with them instead of focusing on their work. The result is that the person who is aware of the weakness often turns to appropriate corrective action. That's what you're missing with your comments. If such a process takes place in the long term, the process that is deposited in your mind will lead you in an unseen direction that you did not think of, in connection with the strong subconscious. Trying to compare your actions with others is the foundation of new attitudes or transforming into a productive person. In case of change, it must be independent. Convincing you that everything was done conservatively as before, depending on conformity with others or criticism of others will not be an initiative for change. The same old things will be repeated to you.

Try to avoid imitating giants or world-famous people who have done great work in certain subjects. It is important to take them as examples or study their actions for your perfect life as a player. However, try to avoid depending 100% on their opinions. From the day you were born into this world, you have a strong path ahead of you. Understand it. To conquer the world, to be happy, to be rich, and to be enlightened are your rights. You must line up and use that path. Get on that path as soon as possible.

All these together should make a new wave of change in your playing. The world is waiting for it to happen. Therefore, you should do it. For this, you must have strong self-confidence and strength. Try to cultivate that spirit. For this, you must develop courage. If you haven't lined up for it yet, start it today. First, you must make your image of the hero within. Place two or three pictures of yourself in your bedroom or the room you hang out in the house most often. If you have pictures of other people or everyone you've ever considered a hero, remove them all. Insert a photo of yourself on the screen of your mobile phone when you open it up in the morning. You love yourself. A change in thinking results in a change in action.

To make a player's journey colorful and meaningful, you should attempt to take further steps forward in your existence as a musician, that lift you up. Focusing on the process of teaching the instrument you have mastered, motivating a group of students to play and gathering them together to hold a free concert once a year, taking the opportunity to enter the stage to show the strength and uniqueness of your playing in live concerts, all will help you for your survival. Launching a lesson or series of lessons for beginners or fans of your mastered instrument on the Internet (YouTube), publishing a booklet about the musical field you have entered with your special knowledge and experience, one or more compositions that include you're playing and creations, your interest in things like publishing on the streaming platforms are also will add light and strength to your playing career. You should think twice about this. You should enter this field with new thinking. The strong foundation you laid, in the beginning, must be condensed and built upon.

Criticism is an analysis of the merits or demerits of work or a person, a work of art or a piece of literature or a piece of music, or any object. This decision maker is called the critic. Likewise, it is important to consider criticism as a decisive exercise in judging the value or value of human existence. When someone says to another, 'You are smart', that is a commentary. This comment is essential for your survival accuracy. A proper understanding of logic, reason, or design is the result of that criticism. A critic of any subject should be a person who has a perfect understanding of the world, people's activities, literature, music, and art in general, and a proper and deep understanding and study of art. Critics who have studied the subject in depth for playing are a separate set of people. The fact is that the criticism is not at all suitable for a player. The damage caused by misjudgments in criticism is enormous. Keep all these aside and line up for the role of a strong player. The role of the critic should be to examine whether a product or design has achieved a service, justice, or progress for society or humanity at large. For this purpose, to analyze the shape of its product value creation and publish an opinion on it should be executed accurately. He should examine the composition of the musician or performer to see how much this piece of music is comforting, enjoyable, or has a meaningful message for the listener. He should pay special attention to the meaning of its strong satisfaction. These two functions are contradictory. Criticism is the socialization of a judgment. Creation is the socialization of satisfaction.

Most of the time people choose a picnic or an educational trip to a place where there are very crowded festivals, processions, places of worship and cities, etc. These create confusing or complex images in our minds and in the long run, this event closes one aspect of your creativity. The mind should be opened widely. It should be associated with a well-opened environment. The wide range of an open mind will make you a giant. You are not alone in an open massive environment. It makes you a free and relaxed person mentally and physically. The player should always be relaxed in mind and body, because his body should be relaxed when playing. A stiff and stressed body will not balance the action of the two hands. A player's life is his two hands. Existence is its strong and well-trained fingers.

It is in these lonely and still moments that your free thoughts arise. Every moment you spend with your musical instrument, its sound lingers in your ears. Try to recognize the combination of silence and sound, the two phenomena of opposite directions. Silence has a very powerful place in the sound. It is difficult for the person who is unable to recognize silence to recognize the sound correctly. Silence has no meaning in the absence of sound. Then you will not recognize the silence.

Every sound is built through silence. Likewise, enter the silence and be still. There is a pause or silence in the sentences used in every conversation. If there is no such silence, the ideas of the speaker will be unclear. Therefore, playing is the same. Any silence involved is mandatory for the survival of the play. In this way, silence is given priority in playing as well as sound.

The mind is powerfully engaged with every moment you practice. Although the physical exertion of the performer is minimal during practice or performing on stage, the mental exertion becomes intense due to the mental connection with the work. Keeping the mental posture strong and balanced is very important currently. Practicing patience is very helpful in maintaining this process successfully.

Never, ever, reveal your plans to anyone before they are put into action. Don't tell your ideas to anybody. Because, with such expression, some people's opinions and anger are often presented and it will directly affect the design in one's mind. About that design, its core will also be damaged and one's identity will be lost. Always be careful not to be a creator of words without action. Work in silence. Focus on your activities so silently. Announcing something before it's launched will make one lose interest in it to some extent. Its depth and expressive power will be somewhat relaxed. The performer's strength lies in his revelations of the past and hope for the future based on that strength. Satisfied with the musician's creations, the listener joins him and embraces him with the belief that he will be a great support and comfort and this thought will be a beneficial factor for the player's journey and to popularize of such creations in the future. Such listeners are a great strength for the player.

Never, ever let the concept of the player slip away from you. Often it happens because the player pursues actions or concepts that are inappropriate or incompatible with his journey. This process causes the listeners of the player to lose interest or love for the player. Never let a player lose sight of his goal. It is meaningful for the survival as a player to engage in the processes that give results to one's playing. Through these processes, the popularity of his playing is determined. The feelings or emotions that arise in the human mind in some cases practically trap the man and it is very harmful to the existence of the man for his behavior and decisions. Therefore, a person who has embarked on a strong journey with strong determination must have a good understanding of this. It is a victory to be consciously aware of this rather than underestimating the biases in decision-making behavior and existence, as nature has inculcated a deceiving process into every relationship. A wise man will also be trapped in these biases. Such incidents are common, especially in the behavior and existence of a player. He achieves his goals not by denying them but by controlling them well. Understanding one's own emotions and one must control those emotions before controlling oneself and understanding the emotions of others is a characteristic of a musician. Or it should be a mastered art of his mind. Mastering arts is an extremely difficult process. If that difficult process is lost in someone's hand, he will be a victim of it. You will be limited in it and trapped in your frame. A smile may acquire a temporary pleasure or a relief, but it will not last forever. Avoid seeing temporary shelters in a player's ever-strong effort. Some people get pleasure from seeing and hearing the pain or suffering in the world. They are oppressed in it. In such a world, the player must say goodbye to such a view. Worrying about the pain and suffering of others is squeezing one's, own soul. It is a gateway to a tragic plane where man has transcended. Such a state is not at all suitable for a player who is in search of a new wave of performance. The sad or defeated thoughts of the past should be erased, and the daydreaming about the future should also be erased. Such a future of a player should emerge as a vision embedded in a powerful framework intertwined with reality. A path will be visible before him that is strongly reinforced in the future, perfected by meaning and reality, where existence and thought are strong. That's how it should be. Every player who represents a powerful instrument must have this kind of strong vision. Stimulation of proper vision is not a prior merit or luck. It is a result of a combination of many painstaking steps.

Representing the role of a player, you have the right to choose different engagements in various fields of career. For example, let's say you are a qualified music teacher. For that career, you wake up in the morning, go to school, teach the music curriculum to the students for five to six hours, finish school, fulfill your role at home (whether you are a man or a woman), and practice your instrument. After getting ready for the next day's teaching lessons, you may spend time with your family members in the evening and watch TV during this time, enjoy dinner together, probably after washing, and go to bed at night. This was the routine of a typical music teacher, and it was also common to have private lessons at home on Saturdays and Sundays. In addition to this, there may be some changes in the daily routine of individuals. Most of the time you will be satisfied with these daily routines. Because you have done your duty due to maintain good relations and fulfill obligations. But if your contribution representing the role of a player is labeled as too common and ordinary, you will surely be disappointed or angry. You, too, along with most of the world's population, have gradually become trapped in a common plane or a framework that represents a common group even without your knowledge. It is tragic. Even though most people like this in the world are satisfied with contributing to the process of maintaining the world through their representation, their effort to change the existence of the world or to enter a new path is not enough at all. What is needed is not to keep the world unchanged. When it needs growth, a step forward, a new concept, or a technology, it's so tragic if you're the only one staying. But most individuals have stayed hand in hand with you. Such a human race is associated with this old conservative wave representing various professions all over the world.

If so, what should be done? Your opposition to the process of change is huge. It is not only in your field, but this reaction is the same in many fields of the world. You will be able to experience or understand many things that you need to change in the future in this book. Thought becomes action. The stronger the thoughts the stronger the action. Establishing such strong thoughts in you must be done first and it is a tough conversation within yourself just like a tug of war. Any person who has been inclined to one direction or behavior for a long time, even if there is an objection to it in his mind, does not hesitate to express it because he has less energy to walk away from it and move into a new direction. Because of their reluctance to break with their long-held identity or habits. Many people live in these ivory towers they have built and say goodbye to their lives in that world. If you hesitate to take this bold step today, you will worry about it one day. That is, it is your twilight time of life that you do not see in your present or old age. If you don't see it nowadays, you may think it's not a weakness, or it's a perception problem of old age. Study the current structure of a few who have reached old age or if you get a chance, take the opportunity to go to an old people's home. Have a chat with some of the elders there. You will understand that more than 90% of their information got to this place because of their poor existence without using proper management or method. Nature, human influences, and certain systems will never line up in your favor. You must build it all on a proper plan with effort. You must prepare for your stability.

Try to paint a picture in your mind of the twilight of your life. You will take that period to a world or a period that is completely different from the current status. Today's friends will become less and less likely to meet as they get older and get sick. There will also be opportunities to die due to the spread of various diseases such as the current severe epidemics. May your beloved husband or wife pass away? Children may go to distant places or foreign countries for education. Although it is a piece of happy news for you, in many cases such students who have gone abroad do not return to their motherland. Then they will say goodbye to you forever. Or they can get married in their homeland and go to distant places for work or residence. This is how you become stand-alone. Today the world has become a very busy place. In that busy society, it is natural that they forget you and lose you from their minds. However, if your identity as a player was portrayed, if you have popularized a new wave of music today, you will not become an invalid coin. Students will flock to you to study new concepts of your new wave. Society will embrace it if your playing is a youthful energetic message even if you are old. You will build a discourse in society. You will be able to protect your value as well as popularity by using various modern social media. With old age, he will have to say goodbye to the profession of a doctor. No matter what level you are in any sport, with the passage of age, it is certain to say goodbye to that sport. With the aging of the subordinates, he will not be able to survive even as a coach in the game. Thus, many people representing many professions in the world must leave their fields with old age, but because the physical energy used by a player is very little, he or she has the good fortune to stay in that field and remember that no other energy is devoted to his playing other than mental fatigue. Hence, the player remains in a very valuable profession, and you should take steps from today to enjoy its proper results.

You live today in a world where many jobs will be lost in the future. Robots and highly advanced machines and new technologies are taking the place of human beings and many professions. Thus, even if the jobs of many professions are lost, with only the player and a few other professions will remain in their professions, with your powerful instrument. A player as a robot doesn't give 100% feel to a listener. Then you have chosen a great career. Even if the profession is great, you must have a good vision and philosophy about how to stay in it.

Early preparation is more important than late. As a player, this setup as mentioned earlier, which you represent, will never be raised to a strong level late in life. It's not next year or next month or next week or today. It must be revealed on the concept of now and this moment. First, understand the power or value of the concept of the present moment. When that is your sole purpose, everything will be swift and orderly. Make it a daily habit. Look back at your progress at the end of years, months, weeks, and days. You will be amazed and delighted. Preserve that enjoyment. It is your life. It's your eternal victory. It is a great force that awakens your existence or soul and finds an unexpected direction.

Progress, excellence, depth, or improvement in a player's playing never comes for free. For that reason, this can be achieved in the player not being an ordinary player but an excellent player. Check out the playing field. A vast majority of players do not realize what level their playing is at present. The listeners will never label them as players. There are only a handful of legends or greats in any field. The new wave or strength of the playing of those few in the field of playing is very different from other playing. Most of the fans fail to enjoy it in the beginning. It should also be recognized with effort. To socialize this type of instrument on the playing field, the player must represent that field for many years. With such effort, your playing will be cherished by fans for many years. Michael Angelo, the world-famous Italian painter (1475 - 1564) was 70 years old when he was invited to paint the basilica in Italy. American inventor Thomas Edison (1847 - 1931) who created electricity, light bulbs, energy machines, and movies, was engaged in successful experiments even at the age of 80. Irishman George Bernard Shaw (1856 - 1950) wrote powerful plays even in his 90s. Colonel Sanders was an American businessman (1890 - 1980) after working in various jobs; he started the KFC business at the age of 65 and became a millionaire in 20 years. Ray Kroc (1902 - 1984) American businessman, at the age of 52 started the world's largest fast-food company, McDonald's and it has become a huge business today. These are some examples of characters that have represented certain fields for a long time and become icons. Many such strong characters in the world deserve to be analyzed separately from others. It became so because each of them socialized creations or ideas that included different or new concepts. After that, a huge number of people in the world followed these concepts. It is common for society to marginalize the elderly. But remember that old age is the age of intelligence and wisdom. Age is just a number. The brain power when you are twenty years is as same as when you are eighty. Therefore, it is sad to say goodbye to action with time. This is the time that a mature person should be strongly connected with a process. Therefore, get out of your lonely environment. Stand up from the reclining chair. This is your time. It's not an illusion. It's an initiative for a great mission as a player.

In any field that pursues such strong goals, the majority will receive or encounter essential ideas and opportunities for effective progress. As a player, when you have embarked on a powerful journey, avoid focusing on or acting on things that do not bring out value or strengths to you. Then the majority will come to you only with such meaningful and effective opportunities and ideas. When you let go of the unimportant for a long time, what remains is always productive. When the water is well filtered, only the necessary clean water will be collected, and the container will be filled.

You should frequently explore your current level or level of playing. For that, it is mandatory to conduct necessary evaluations and be aware of the current level of other players playing and what level you are currently in comparison with their playing. Avoid using your parents, relatives, close friends, or boyfriend or girlfriend for this test, because due to the closeness of this group to you, proper criticism will not be expressed about your playing or creations. In this way, they may be a group of people who do not know well about music and your creations. Especially because of the strong affection and love that parent have for their children; it is natural not to express such weaknesses even if they see them. They will never try to upset you and will make sure that you are comforted at every moment. The same goes for other relatives, friends, or fiancés.

After a long time of being satisfied with your playing with the reviews of those without such knowledge and experience, it may be too late to change or build something again. This will negatively affect your playing career by building strong anxiety about your abilities. Therefore, employ persons who have good knowledge about music and composing. Ask for reviews from several persons, not just one person because they hear different aspects of your playing.

Most in society are not ready to accept when someone declares their shortcomings or weaknesses. Criticizing the person who made a critical statement is also common. So, it is useless to get angry or try to claim that the criticism is not correct when an expert criticizes, your playing. Then there is no point in you representing this field. What a meaningful, productive, deep, and beautiful place the world would be if everyone representing every sector of the world was right. Why wouldn't it be? As such comments and corrections are not always done correctly because such reviews are rare in the world.

A strong individual always follows a strong thought. He will reap the fruits of that thought. In the same way, it is natural for any strong person that other people to respect him or obey his opinion and follow him. It has been happening throughout the history of the world. So, as a musician, it's only natural that you have a following and gather as fans. But for that to happen there must be a change or a new wave in your playing. There must be a message in the music that the listener has not heard before. Being followed by a group and fans following you will bring out the idea that you have accomplished something new in the world. That is exactly what should happen. One should add something meaningful to the world in one's lifetime. It is for the survival of the world and its growth. The happiness and the thought process that the performer receives with this will lift him a few more steps for the rest of his life, and his service and work will go down in history as an immortal service to the field of music. To manage human life purely or strongly for pleasure without sorrow is the right existence. That is the goal that every man aspires to.

Passionate about your inner human strengths is the most powerful resource for survival. To cultivate it, you must dedicate yourself from a young age. Its truth helps to move one to desired heights and to stay away from the concept of heavy dependence on material resources. By chasing material resources, the player will lose his thoughts about human resources and will be caught in the competition that the world has built for material existence. Traveling in a car is not reflected in the world as wealth. Also walking does not reflect poverty. The performer must be a character full of mental powers beyond that. No matter what field you represent in the world, being strong with inner human energy helps you to be at the top of that field. Every moment your inner human energy is strong, you will have the power to control not only your mind, discipline, and proper existence but also control every event you face by using that energy. This is the reason why many strong people do not hesitate to make certain decisions without anyone's help or knowledge. They always have solutions for all the challenges that arise in front of them. After the rainy season, the drought will come. That drought is also temporary. The rainy season is coming again.

Your strongest defense is intelligence. It protects you and your well-controlled existence. No one will go near the fire. The harm caused by it is well known. Even one mentally retired, will not touch the fire. That control is intelligence. Even if someone has experienced stress, the intelligence has not diminished. Therefore, in making certain decisions, intuition informs you about the immediate decision. You will have the strength to solve any problem or challenge that comes your way. Because intelligence with such a strong foundation and depth not only controls you well for that task but also takes you to the desired step or plane in your life. Life can be managed well by focusing on the right decisions. That way you can step into the desired plane or direction.

It is natural for the composer to see or experience nature, the separation of love, defeat, old age, sorrow, or pleasure conceived in his mind. You must be smart in making such a concept into a composition for the rapidly changing modern society. But in it you should not insult old age, turn love's separation into an exaggeration, praise poverty beyond the limit, nor reveal such things as deep sorrow. Probably your compositions may confirm the opinion of modern philosophers who claim that the essence of beauty and content is not visible or only at a very low level in modern art, music, architecture, and literature. It is timely if concepts that awaken energy, intelligence, and a new way of thinking for human existence or the survival of society are included in your creations.

If you don't build your identity by giving what everyone expects or asks for, it's just an empty confusing web that has no meaning in one's existence. Is it one's existence? What is Life? Is it an empty jumble of confusion without meaning? It is your job to add meaning to life to build your identity during your lifetime and for the sake of humankind. Its importance is highlighted by the depth or meaning contained in it, therefore, the true meaning of life that separates from the common and opens to new meaningful concepts constructs meaning and departs from life in a meaningful way.

From the beginning of history, world-renowned and powerful philosophers expressed their views to the world. Even though those opinions were conflicted in the beginning, they have become the truth or reality today. Because of that, the world has transformed into great growth and change in various fields. So, you are one member of the world who can do this. This work must be done by you. That should be your job or duty as a representative of the world. You didn't come to this world to end life the way everyone lives. You were sent to this world for one powerful task. That's what you got the membership for. That's a rare membership. Although many people have no idea about it, it is the truth. As a player or as a composer it's a must.

FIRST STEP

Chapter 2

"You have come to this world for mighty work,
Get it done".

Musical instruments trace their history back to the 6th century (BC). The journey since then has ranged too far to be written or discussed. Performance is an act using a musical instrument whether on a stage, theater, or outdoor venue, performing for others' enjoyment or satisfaction. Its medium is sound. Today, the field of playing a musical instrument has become very professional and it has become one of the most powerful businesses in the world, involving massive amounts of money.

This book explains to the reader that the new waves [new genres] of playing are coming continuously from the beginning of the sixth century. Thus, if we divide the world of music according to periods, we can see how much it has been changing from the beginning. In the same way, it can be revealed that the composer's playing styles came into the limelight along with new waves.

From the year 1950 until the present day, there are a huge number of musicians and composers of musical styles born in the world. It is very difficult to publish an in-depth analysis or presentation of those in a book that provides information for a new wave of players, and it will be clear how fast musical styles are being introduced to the world. During such rapid transformations, it is important that you, as a player, join the bandwagon and understand what you will experience if you do not join hands with the new wave. This book is a preparation for that. Often due to certain activities in society, it is natural for man to look for different aspects and make transformations. Stepping into discoveries is a very smart thing to do. Or stepping into a chasing wave and creating your wave from it is also a successful solution. Your future or future existence will be determined by your association with either of these two steps. It is a crucial moment. People representing many different fields who have made tough decisions like this have pursued their goals and become world-ranked as the best in that field. All these great people are ordinary people like you and there is no difference in the minimum facilities, resources and activities they have had at the beginning. You must follow them within your given facilities and opportunities. But the lack of exploration based on understanding may be very tragic.

Remember, every time you face a defeat or a setback, or some serious loss, you will be followed by a serious and meaningful new conception that is fueled by that event. You don't have to be always observant to understand this. Because this process is about reaching you with something stronger than what you have imagined. Therefore, stick to your process.

Opportunities like these will arise for anyone optimistic about their future. As one door closes another opens. The new concept or opportunity that opens will be very effective for you and will be a suitable foundation for an unexpected step forward. So don't worry about failures or losses. Keep in mind that this kind of thing only comes to a human being that is looking for success and strength. No matter what part of the world you live in, it can be a very crowded city, or it could be a small village away from a busy society in solitude. Today, man has managed to travel every corner of the world. The technology and transportation of the world are so far ahead. But the thought of a person living in an isolated village is whether it is possible to go to any part of the world from such a place. Thus, you are at an unknown or slow level because you are not at a strong level as stated earlier and because the one who is at such a strong level has taken all available opportunities to convert such strengths into his achievements. You must build the strength or such an environment for yourself.

The process of life is a chain of moves forwarding gradually in line with one another. Meanwhile, you will constantly be overwhelmed by the changes and what needs to be accomplished. You will also be concerned about understanding and transforming the change. Often the change will reach you in a way you did not expect. Therefore, the accidental occurrences that face the player and the composer in his journey through these breakdowns and transformations are a great relief.

Therefore, when the time comes, don't be afraid or sad to let go of certain relationships, say goodbye to certain places, or part with a certain process. During that time, you should study the task wisely and separate. You rarely get a chance for such a transformation. You should accept it at that moment and such events will arise for an event that directly affects your existence or your career. But the reason for regret is that the majority will give up such opportunities and try not to separate from the status quo which became a pressure for them. It means that you hesitate to build change or fresh concepts into your being. Concepts don't just develop. You must build them with effort.

By saying goodbye like that, you might face setbacks or defeat. Such setbacks or defeats are a slight hindrance to the strength of your playing career. The society also assesses your worthiness based on tough decisions like these. As in any other field, there are many setbacks and drastic changes in the playing career. It should be so and must be denied the uniformity of its existence.

You've heard of people who have worked in one place for years until they retired. His or her remuneration level is based on their position and promotions. Such should be the pattern of that profession. But a player's existence is never like that. He should establish human relations in different places of society at different times. It is good if he or she changes the living environment and place and society from time to time. You must act as soon as you come to such a situation. The player should not stay for a long time in one place until he gets old. If so transformations of his existence in his career may not happen. Based on the existence of the environment, your thinking will go to different aspects and new concepts and ideas will be generated in you. Those transformations will directly affect your playing or creations.

When one is sad, happy, defeated, or awarded, completely contradictory emotions, new ideas and concepts will arise. Likewise, when you change the province or geographical location where you live and work, your ideas, which have been uniform for a long time, will take a different form. That change will directly affect your creativity or existence in a meaningful way. Those transformations may largely and meaningfully affect your compositions and your existence. Even if your style is the same, it should highlight different new patterns and concepts. In the long run of monotony, the appreciation of your work is lost in the hands of the listener. Not only should you retain your audience permanently, but you should also be able to integrate new listeners into that group. It will never happen in a uniform pattern. This change is simply for the betterment of the player. In this way, he or she goes through different ranges and acquires many meaningful things in this journey. Life is never in one place. The player must think that there are no permanent shelters on his journey. If you get a chance to participate in a concert held in a foreign country or a new playing opportunity, you must take it, it is very valuable experience. The experience you acquire in a different culture in a different society is a very strong factor in the survival of the playing career. Once you have affixed the label of a player to your career, you must follow a process that takes it to higher levels. A mandate is rare. It is even more difficult to maintain such a mandate.

Approach the challenging things in life. Then there are many new concepts, you can learn from facing difficulties. This will highlight your existence or your strength and there is nothing in this world that you will gain or acquire by joining or connecting with ordinary things or people. Such members are abundant in the world or society. They see no difference. They are afraid of facing changes or setbacks. They clash with the common crowd and finally leave this world. A player or a stalwart in any of such professions should not be like that. That's sad.

Life is a meaningful journey that should be faced with challenges and progress with the resources of happiness and success with proper management. It affects not only a player but every other field. 'Man must find happiness and use proper management for its existence.' The world-famous Greek philosopher Aristotle pointed out.

In society, you have often heard that a person or a group is led by one person. Or you may have seen such. If such a person is lost in the hands of the person that person or group will get lost. That person or group remains temporarily in the field, and it is impossible to tell at what moment their collapse will occur. They have become puppets. They stand like a machine and have no idea or plan for innovation or change. Sadly, such a character will not discover a new wave [genre] of the player. Because to create a new wave, it is important to include a strong procedure in him, and thoughts and concepts that seek a different way for the new creation are mandatory. No one can take such a step relying on the advice and control of others.

You must understand what you think and want in the player for a new wave. When what we think and want changes, so does our action. Therefore, you must transform yourself into a different path or vision. For this, a deep understanding of music and musical patterns must be acquired by staying in the field for a long time. You must stay firm on the theme of this change or new pattern. That's how you should use it. This is the moment where the conflict between society and the listener begins. The many listeners who have embraced you (not all, but some) may leave you. But keep in mind that dropouts will eventually reconnect with you with time. Or a new group will join hands with you.

However, a certain group of listeners will say goodbye to you forever with this change. Do not be nervous. No one in the world can please everyone. Attempts to do so are bound to fail. Man is different. Likewise, certain events and facts are looked at from different angles. If so, leave that group. Few in the world come close to something deeply meaningful. How rich is it if you're playing conveys something so deep, powerful, original or meaningful? How valuable is it to your survival? The main reason for this is that your change or new style is serious or rather difficult for them to understand and they will reconnect as their listening and understanding powers become stronger. It is natural for the listener to get tired and frustrated by hearing the same thing repeatedly. They will understand your conversion as any change in his listening tendency will happen over time. As many things are changing in society, he is expecting this change in playing as a result of his engagements with such changes. In the beginning, many unpleasant and unclear things become clearer and more meaningful with time. It is human nature.

Over time, some of the listeners who left because of the new wave of your playing will refuse to come back to you. Don't be shocked about it. Such characters are few in society. They are a group of stubborn people who will not change. You must reject them. By telling the world his identity which cannot be changed or embraces transformations, he is expecting some individuality from society. They may call him heroic. Reject such people. Because you don't want to waste time trying to convince them. Use your valuable time for some other meaningful activity. He does not act according to his wisdom and tries to stand out by showing his needs to society by sticking to firm decisions. It is also important that such people reject many things that they cannot do due to the weakness that they are not able to rally for such a change or a new trend. They criticize most things due to their lack of understanding of new patterns and new concepts. They never develop an interest in such new changes.

New ways are mandatory for the progression or continuation of the performer. If the new trends, new concepts, and new waves are not born with time musical instruments will be rejected from the field with time. In this way, when you study the musical instruments that were left in the field in the past, you will understand these reasons well. Some players may not like to establish a new wave. They may believe the existence of my musical instrument must be eternally unchanged. In thinking of it like that, the progress of the musical instrument or its retention without separation from the field will never happen. Man's thoughts or thinking changes. It is also different. The monotonous style of playing gets lost in the hands of listeners with time and they expect a change. Therefore, a new trend of an instrument is needed.

During the Renaissance, Baroque and Classical eras, the musicians used only their compositions for their performances for about 95% of the time and it concluded till the end of the 19th century. After that, many musicians used other composers' compositions for their concerts or performances, which was one of the main reasons for the setback of new creations.

The need for a new concept or trend of music is repeatedly expressed in this book to keep the instrument alive. After all, if such a change does not happen, the instrument's playing style will be uniform. Then the people who liked that style of playing will move to a different style due to monotony and a new generation with new ideas and concepts will not join this old and stalled style.

Today, the mobile phone in the hand of people, and the computer carried in their bags have become essential items. They are all deeply close to those goods. Without such closeness, they have no existence. Because of one's work, one's existence, knowledge, new technology, and many processes are carried out using these. It is natural that their thoughts or thinking changes with time while dealing with such modern technology tools. This group is a large group of people in the world. A huge number of the world's population. Unsurprisingly, such a generation is not satisfied with the old conservative or monotonous sound patterns. They will develop a concept that this change in their thinking should be included in everything else in society. Furthermore, many things like modern architecture, modern vehicles, modern clothing styles, and modern furniture, have been created in the present day there, as expected by their thought ears, or eyes. Many of them are devoted to listening to music. It is simply used as relaxation, comfort, enjoyment, or escape from loneliness and they would expect this novelty or new wave to be established in the music they are listening to. If this change in everything is not in the music they listen to, they will not be satisfied with it and look for new trends. The facts are that there must be a change or a new trend in the music or the playing of the instrument you are skilled in for its existence.

Today, as in the past, musical styles, and musical instruments are gradually declining in popularity and use. The main factors are the lack of new players entering the field, the uniformity of the musical instrument, the uniformity of the style, and the lack of diversity or transformation in the styles used by certain popular players. Likewise, another strong factor is the technological transformation, as critics point out that musical compositions that used electronic instruments are very much in that place.

Any sound or musical performance produced by a radio, or a recording released on the Internet (streaming platforms) entices you to listen to them. In a live performance, in a hall, at a festival, on the street, or on a road, a musician's performance is with value and provides satisfaction. For the listener, if there is no pattern in the action and playing of the performer, a problem will arise, and the meaning of the performance will be diminished. The very meaning of the live performance will then become collapsed. Therefore, no matter how popular and marketed artificial or electronic instruments are in the world, even if such musical instruments are electronic, on a concert stage, or on a television channel, they must be played by a player. Even if a robot performs the instrument, the core is bound to break, so the player must perform his instrument even in a concert or a pre-recorded television program. Thus, no matter how much technology and tools in the world are advanced, a player will forever enjoy a better existence than many representing other fields. His career will never end because people today have increased a lot more than before to watch live concerts. We can see this from the high cost of the tickets for concerts by famous singers and musicians. Therefore, whatever changes occurred in the original and traditional concepts of the field of music, the decision made, to line up for becoming a professional player is a worthwhile investment.

Due to the powerful technological transformation that took place in the 20th century, with the use of computers and mobile phones from childhood to youth, their minds have become less creative. The use of modern goods including advanced technology and AI was the main reason for reducing the conception of thoughts that had a new aesthetic value in the mind. By pressing a few buttons on the computer and handling it well, one can achieve the needs of the computer, but in the creation of a piece of music, one's technical knowledge, thinking power, emotions, mood or taste, experiences, knowledge of music and understanding of theories are mandatory for that creation. With the long-term use of the tools of technology, his hands will gradually lose what is needed for the creation. It may have been directly influenced by the drastic transformation of architecture, fashion, automobiles, roads, and everyday tools in their living environment. Therefore, it is not surprising that today's youth are getting closer to the music produced by using such electronic equipment.

Your musical instrument may be combined with a well-known style that exists in the world today and by playing that style well you will gain popularity. No matter how strong you are in playing the instrument, if that playing style is not your own playing style or that style declines in popularity one day, you who used that style will also be in trouble. Therefore, always try to bring out a difference in whatever style of music you play. Your survival as a player will be determined by these changes you make.

According to global reports made by the world's most powerful institutions, the world's music industry has been profitable as an industry for seven consecutive years, and in 2022 alone, global recorded music revenues reached $31.2b. Global streaming revenues reached 20 billion U.S. dollars in the same year. In 2023 three major music companies in the world earn 2.9 million revenues per hour. Thus, world music is growing as an industry while some musical instruments are declining in popularity and use.

It is not so easy for the youth as newcomers to enter the highly competitive music industry in today's world. The situation is sad if they are hoping to represent the field as a performer. Because the player needs more than the playing ability, they must also have money for their propaganda and strong connections for a successful journey. Today, many colleges and institutes are preparing youths for this kind of situations in the West. Some of these institutions are run for free. The main reason for that is to bring new people into this field and keep it running continuously without collapse. Likewise, this also makes them aware of the modern music industry and its new trends.

According to modern philosophers, today most of the arts (fine arts) are creations without artistry and beauty. Those designs only try to express their individuality and it is questionable how meaningful the message is. The message contained in the music must be modern, and it must contain a nature compatible with other products, ideas, and services emerging in the world.

Man has directly contributed too many changes or transformations in the world and thus the transformation has become mandatory for the betterment of every human being in the world. Certain changes, improvements or developments or new products, etc. in the field he represented have all contributed to this. It has made the world meaningful and prosperous.

Therefore, the field of music that you represent is also the same. Your contribution to it is mandatory for its continuous and innovative development. He must make such a transformation in a field where anyone is representative. Then the world will take a step forward every moment.

Your process will be tailored according to your need and interest. The process does not happen as soon as such needs arise in you. For that, you need to launch a good start as well as a strong plan for it. Gradually the thought of necessity will begin to function meaningfully as you pursue it. This will take some time, because you will learn lot during that time. In the hasty, fast pursuit, you will miss out on many things as well as slip away from your hands, so calm down. Always allow the thoughts of your priorities to move into a wider range. Be aware and rally around those thoughts. Over time many things will slowly catch up to you or even overtake you. That way you will build new relationships. New ideas will be implemented. The search will line up before you how to build it meaningfully. Thus, you should come forward for a new wave of playing without any reluctance or doubt.

Not everything is competitive. When that kind of competitiveness is established in you, what you need to grasp will slip away from you. Competition should be established within you and only with yourself. Competition in your field in the world is natural today. It remains the same in any field. You should explore it without competition. Every human being in the world has the right and the ability to live continuously or successfully in any social system and culture. Keeping your rights in mind, you should look for the necessary procedure or method to get into it and stay in the field. You have the rights, but the methods are different. You must study and find out what they are, and it will take a lot of intelligence and exploration to implement your new way. Sometimes the progress made for your actions may be very small. Don't think about it that way. Small things are important for your growth. A lot of such small things add up and eventually, the big thing builds up in front of you.

The environment around you, the people, and the day-to-day events are embedded in many things that develop one's journey. Therefore, you should strengthen your steps to get rid of them and achieve your goals. Events like this are not limited to you. It is common. If not, everyone in the world would be far ahead of what you see today. The strong people of the world have occupied those positions by clashing with the forces with long-term commitment. Therefore, such a character will not be born instantly.

VALUE OF THE NEW WAVE OF PLAYING

Chapter 3

"You should do something permanent in playing. Change must also be embedded in it for longevity".

Humans need change or transformation for growth or meaningful existence. It doesn't do well in the same level for a long time. Therefore, he is tempted to experiment. When there is no progress in that change, another method is used again. A change in clothes, a change in food, a change in the environment, a change in friendship, a change in the house, a change in the office, a change in one's image or shape, haircut, shoes, clothes, body color, etc. will greatly influence this. He continues this process by experimenting. Regardless of the field, you are in, we have experienced that if discoveries and new methods are not used the product or service will fail at some point. It has become fashionable for humans to be attracted to modern or different things. It has become a must to innovate.

Given these facts, if you own a label as a player, it is timely to do an in-depth study of the above-mentioned facts. It is a strong point that has an effect anywhere in the world. You must line up for that. If your conversion does not happen, the audience will leave you. There is nothing more tragic in your field than not having an audience. The listener expects a transformation or a change in yours because of the transformation he experiences physically or mentally by encountering society. It is natural for him to seek solutions to various problems, transformations, and mental pressures faced in society. As a result, from literature, music, and cinema, and in general, through aesthetics, he seeks relief. There is a very close relationship between the relief sought and the transformation taking place in society. As a result, your monotonous music pattern is not the solution to his problems. If he is not satisfied with your playing, he must find relief from another player. For this there are huge numbers of players in the world. It is natural for a patient to leave the doctor if that patient does not recover. If you do a good study, you will realize how the most conservative things fade away from people's minds and practices with time. Meanwhile, relationships, thoughts wish, civilization and culture also fade away.

Many books are published in the world every day, and no matter what language they are written in, as soon as there is a new method or a new concept of change in expressing ideas or handling the language, the value of that book will get a strong demand while the sales increases. The ideas contained in it will tempt you to read it not once but several times. Why is that so? Because the reader did not get a chance to hear or read that idea or thought before. This transformation is bound to happen when new concepts are added to your playing. The man was ready and willing to be inclined toward new ideas. All that is required is that you fulfill that need. How this happens in music will be discussed in the next chapters.

It is not appropriate for you to make the actors (its characters) in cinema or characters in novels or famous singers as heroes or imitate those characters. It is not suitable for you who are looking for a new wave of playing, as well as for anyone who is looking for a transformation or a change in any other field. By that, you will seriously damage your identity. You are a special person. Character, intelligence, speech, and walking are unique in their way. Therefore, there is no other person like you in this world. Avoid comparing yourself with others immediately. It is a strong barrier to expressing your identity. Be keen to take your place in this world first. Understand it. Imitation is necessary for some creations. But it is only within certain limits.

Representing thc role of a player, depending on your present age, you are likely to stay in the field for at least thirty to forty or fifty years or even more with your playing career. Every person in the world strives to live longer. Especially with aging, old age or late life is very concerned about good health. As you get older and mature, you should be interested in staying active in the field. You have seen that various products in the market have been at the forefront of the world, competing for many years. For that, those companies will use intensive modern and well-planned advertising. For you to stay in the field for a long time, such a market or such a system is essential for its long existence. In the meantime, it is very appropriate to get out of the monotony of your playing and enter a change or a new trend that is repeatedly expressed in this book, and for that, it is important to line up in advance. In the 1950s or 1960s, the changes in some areas were slow, but today the changes are happening very quickly and fast. Therefore, it is imperative to make a meaningful effort to stay in your market. Some are afraid to change many things that are hereditary or traditional. Otherwise, there are cases where there is no right in certain traditions to change that tradition. But when one looks at the past or history, one realizes that many of those traditions or conservative things have fallen out of use in society. The result of forcefully preserving or perpetuating a tradition is its gradual disappearance from society. Tragically, a small group of people who tried to preserve certain things through a legal system or by striving is living detached from society.

An average number of people do not show any appetite for such changes, and it is a common process for them to criticize those who seeking to create that change. Take the various products available in the world as an example. The people who advertise things that's essential to human life such as houses, vehicles, furniture, technology tools, food, drinks, clothes, etc. When you study the actions taken by those companies, you see the highly competitive nature of these businesses has meant that its advertising methods have also needed to take a new formula and there are unimaginable methods used in this. Even if you play the role of a quiet player, through the study of those methods, you will also acquire an understanding of such modern methods and it will help you in your future journey.

Expressing opposition to certain changes in any field is a common practice of some individuals in society. The main reason for this is to condemn others when they do something they cannot do. But using the procedure contained in this book will guide anyone who declares that "I am weak, I can't, and my knowledge is little", to use the appropriate and important methodologies that can be implemented to develop a new wave of playing. As a reminder, anyone in the world (unless they have a mental disorder) is very capable and at a level where they can build perfection in their field. Be keen to understand it quickly and thoroughly. Life is not for suffering. It is for building a strong and meaningful existence. First, you must understand it. Get out of imitating others. Avoid criticism. Don't let the goals slip away. Decide for this today or at this moment. Get started right now. This is the perfect moment. Don't let the depth of your life or its purpose slip away from you. Don't be late. Tomorrow is not the best day. Not in the future. Now is the perfect moment for that.

The competition in the world is very high in any fields today, but in the music field, new players must come forward for a change, if it is not the case, the emergence of certain gaps in the field will cause a risk, even if it is quite difficult to research or explore, it has become a task that must be done. The world's biggest businesses are constantly bringing new products to the market. It is always sent to the market and happens continuously, but it is very rare for a player in the front of the field to use more than one style and release other styles in addition to that style. That change or the new trend is necessarily only done by a beginner or a new player. Popular music is always young people's business and young generation must join the field of music. This new player or player with a new trend studies the present field of music and introduces it to the market. The player selects an uncommon style. Therefore, the entry of new young players who have achieved a new trend is a great strength to the field and prevents the collapse of the field.

In the 1950s and 1960s, a person with a bachelor's degree, a job, a house, a car, a wife, and children were considered a perfect citizen of a country where that person had acquired all the meaning of an accomplished life. But today it has been reflected in front of the world that many of these resources are just ordinary and not extravagant. So much so that today's world has transformed into a complex and multi-step forward era. Same as music is also undergoing changes and has faced some transformations today. Modern music industry also very complicated. It happened without dictating, and every new product invention in the world has been transformed in this way. That process is changing. This change is continuously progressing with the entire universe evolving and if one does not join with that change, one will suffer some setbacks.

Whatever musical instrument you have mastered, realize that through that instrument you possess an amazing power and that you can do some mighty amazing things with that power that others cannot see. For this, you must spend many years with your mastered instrument. As soon as such an expert picks up his instrument, the listener will feel it, but you will not sense it. That is its nature. There are many things you can do within that limit. Whatever you play will be a piece of meaningful music. The foundation for your long journey should be further strengthened without stopping there. As a musician, don't be satisfied with the status quo. You must go beyond the limits. Let go of the advice of being content with, as taught in many philosophies. There are no limits to growth. For this, the sky will be your end or limit. You will acquire this power at some point. Until that point, you should continue to work closely with your instrument. This is the moment that you have stepped into a broader range. The wave or change you are looking for should be easy for you from here and you should have an idea to undergo some changes in it. For your mind to accept this, you must suggest it to your mind thoroughly. That way, the idea, purpose, or goals you are looking for will come towards you with change over time. You must think of the change. Then the change will be visible in front of you. Then all the subconscious senses will be activated and the new spirit you have been looking for will come alive from the moment you pick up the mastered instrument. It is not a wonder or a mystical effect, but as mentioned before, it is this natural change that unfolds through a combination of thought and musical instruments that you expect. Understand thoroughly that every moment the sound of your instrument blends with the space, the powerful principles of music such as harmony, rhythm, and color in the concept that comes to life in the human mind from the union of the sound of the space and the instrument have an invisible as well as unknowable energy that joins with that human mind.

It is important that you're playing contains an authentic style that is infused with the realities of the new wave. Then it will be accepted as a work preserving the principles that should be contained in music with a deep message. Philosophically, according to St. Augustine who lived in the latter half of the Roman Empire (354 – 430 AD), said organizing or controlling sounds is called music; [music affected the soul and thus, could influence and determine the ethics, action and morals of humans was his main idea] if music is the control or arrangement of the sound in such a way that one enjoys it, then establishing these above theories in your work makes sense. In the same way, including a powerful message that you can add to the listener's life will sustain you're playing. Every day man is looking forward to new concepts, new variations, new friendships, and relationships. Therefore, it's no wonder they're drawn to your playing with this new message in your music. You should not only properly understand the use of resources, but also prepare them properly while promoting them in society. Then, upon successful capture of the listener, you will enter the desired plane.

At first, you might think that such meaningful and profound things are very difficult. It's not surprising either. You, who represent the role of the player, must get rid of such narrow ideas and mindsets. The difficult things in the world become difficult and impossible for the people who cannot escape from that grip and join the easy common society. You are now escaped from that group. You are connected to everything contained within the group you are now in. You are now a perfect man with a new attitude. Understand it. Don't let such values acquired during the long journey be lost. They are as strong as rocks and strong as iron. Not breakable objects like glassware or pottery. No one can destroy them and do not think that you have achieved a miracle. Not even a shadow of illusion or mysticism has touched every particle of reality. Most of the time listener does not understand exactly what he hears. But you must give him satisfaction and a message through what he hears. That is the role of the player.

No one can take away from you the knowledge and ability you acquire based on your thorough knowledge of your instrument, knowledge of music theory, and especially knowledge of traditional and contemporary musical styles. Likewise, it is very timely that you should think carefully about its use and analyze how you should socialize it as a reality. All the above is now in your hands. It is the result of a long journey. It is no secret that the journey was difficult for you, or it was a journey full of experiences. So how fortunate are you to have such a powerful process in your hands? Now you can reap the benefits. This powerful belief is the moment that begins the creation within you without even realizing it. You will generate the strength to feel better about this. It is not difficult at all to use it properly. Do not have any doubt or fear about it. Because with such doubt and fear embedded in your subconscious mind, many of the things mentioned above, will naturally come to a stagnated situation. Such doubt or fear does not control the subconscious mind. It will take you in an unexpected direction. Therefore, overcome all this and thoroughly understand how to build the new wave of your playing by combining the resources you have built with the passion you have now and build the level you should be. Strive for this effort every moment you hold your instrument. A strong person in any field has a product that has contributed to his career, but he must have the ability to handle it differently, socially beneficial, or with new concepts. Further have the experience of seeing the instrument differently from this moment. Many things flow to you now. It's the difference in your playing that you've been waiting for so long. Don't give up on it. Get started now. Not tomorrow. Not even today. Now is the perfect time for that. Establish within yourself the power of the word now. For someone like you, it is a powerful weapon of survival. With the addition of depth to your life, you will have incredible strength. In the same way, to have a Streaming Platform is a jewel or a player of any level. It shows your identity or the depth of your playing career. Therefore, having a performance at this stage of your journey as a musician is a process that sets you up for a refined and solid assessment of your playing career. It is invaluable for your concerts. The number of new fans who connect with you after may want to listen to your performance again. There, you're playing on the internet streaming platforms such as YouTube is a good comfort for them. Having such connections will make the listener forever embrace you're playing and build a conversation with others about it. This way you can earn money through those plays and get great free publicity. Today, in a world where the use of CDs is decreasing, you can connect with various organizations on the Internet (music streaming platforms and YouTube) by connecting to new technology or the latest methods and distributing your music to the world you can earn money.

Such plans are essential to your playing career, and you need to manage those plans well over time. The player entering another process without being a player is an empty existence, and he has not properly understood the essence of that life, and he must enter a solid, deep, and meaningful level that takes fruitful steps to cover that empty existence. For these tasks, some exploration of other prominent players is important, but do not imitate them 100 percent. Firstly, you need a thorough study about your playing style, the country you live in, the quality of your performances, your fans, etc.

In your journey, looking further ahead or recognizing the vision you see must always be a step ahead. This event is your journey towards gradual growth and should be willing to collect all the side affects you encounter there, whether they are less or strong. Although thinking that very small things are not important, even those small things through accumulation will help to build a strength that you did not think of. Thus, you become more powerful and there is new progress that you are looking forward to. As one's action becomes stronger, one will unexpectedly possess something that one desires. So is your life as a player. There is no end to this continuous flowing process. By neglecting or denying it, the rhythmic flow is halted. It happens only when you try to undermine the existence and progress of the playing career. Do not turn away your eye for another task. If that happens, it is a denial of your existence as said before. If you say this is impossible in the journey of the performer, then he should leave the field and make room for others to maintain it or enter it. Such people will be harmful to any field. Approach changes without focusing on results. Then the change or result you are looking for will build up right in front of you.

In composing, there is some imitation involved in every product, every process in the world. Without that imitation, no new or different products or designs are born. Therefore, for the new wave of your playing, try to bring out many new concepts through some imitation. The color turns thoughts. A gentle breeze or a slight breeze brings a pleasant thought to you. So is love, mercy, kindness, or sorrow. All these have contributed to human creation from the beginning of history. You also have the right to follow it. But keep in mind that your identity must be included in that simulation. Your audience will instantly recognize the thought or style of another composer in your composition. You have experienced many such creations and the responses to them are very minimal and the meaningful journey you have launched as a performer will also be undermined. But if you strive to highlight your uniqueness without imitating, the result is that you will receive a strong response to it. Without having to study the playing styles of other players, you can highlight them by using your strong techniques on the instrument you have mastered. Take a small pebble on the ground. Study it carefully by rotating it several times in various directions. You will feel a delicate touch on your fingertips, a shape, and a color that you have not imagined or seen. If possible, break it open and experience the color and form inside. Inside is a color pattern you haven't seen before. Because you have not seen it before, the new concepts in it will create a meaningful concept in your mind. It is the beginning of a new creation. It is a moment when the most suitable concepts blend with the sound of your instrument flow. Try to visualize it in your playing. The position of a thing, its color, its shape, as well as its brightness and sound are closely related. It will recognize the instrument you have mastered. Until you understand this properly, you cannot contribute creatively to building your concept without imitating. Many things flow into life. You should embrace only what makes sense out of it. Reject everything else. For example, it is natural for people to be shocked by various tragic events in society. But such a view is harmful to you. While it's perfectly natural to be shocked by hearing so many tragic things, it's damaging to let it continue to flow through your playing career. When you are a true artist, it is natural to laugh when you are happy, cry when you are sad, and be confused in the face of complexity. You can't go beyond that. If that happens, you will inadvertently lose the role you represent. Don't try to get rid of the composers' balanced thoughts. You are ready for a new wave of a player. The playing is strong, but the new trend is a challenge for you. If you don't find your new wave in front of two such powerful tasks, you will feel like your field has not been recognized, by staying somewhere temporarily or permanently. Have you ever seen such people representing different sectors of society? You are determined to rally for a new wave. You have now entered the field of performing. No one's dream of a new wave will ever become a reality when entering that realm. You should enter the concept of the new trend with strength.

In any field, a strong person or a company, business or economy is concerned about bringing the product to a higher standard based on quality, taste, shape, color, etc. than the previous situation for the people. It should be so. It should be the same for the progress of one's business and the betterment of the world. Therefore, if the profession was chosen as a player, this difference should be established in it as well. It will be considered that one should fulfill to the society or the world. That is the service that must be performed by the player. The performer must perform it, even if the people do not expect it. If so, on the last day of the player's life, he will be able to leave the world free and fearless. How meaningful is it to say goodbye to life? Shouldn't the musician aim to convey a meaningful message without being a burden to the world? No matter how many material resources a man has or how much he acquires, it cannot have any meaningful effect on society. That way he won't be a messenger to society. Isn't the performer's role in life to engage in such a process with meaningful enjoyment that is beneficial to him? Although many of the world's most powerful players used material resources at a high level, the reasons for reaching that level were due to the privileges received by that playing.

The notion that a player should appear as a great person in a time that strives to create a new wave should be rejected. For that new trend, you just need to follow a different style of playing from other players. For this, there is no need to be a perfect person with strong intellectual capacities. All that is required is a wealth of knowledge about the instrument you have mastered a good understanding of the theory, and an understanding of the patterns formed by music. When these three factors are aligned, no one will be able to prevent the creating of the new wave of music. It is already lined up and all that needs to happen is implementation. Sadly, people often do not have a proper understanding of their abilities and strengths. Therefore, a person who has this knowledge has only to start an effort for a new wave or an experiment by utilizing time. Among the abilities, controlling one's musical instrument well or playing powerfully is the most important ability and function for this task. The thought that appears in front of you without any effort is childish and only with effort and much experience will make that thought a reality. The world needs to see that your ideas are rare. It should be demonstrated through effort. Then the listener will immediately experience the value of that effort. A common talent or common idea is not immediately embraced by the listener because it is a common perception that they often experience. There is no idea or opinion that such performance has ever existed in society for a long time.

There should not be a struggle for birth. To express an idea or a concept, there must be an alignment, which will reveal a new emergence. For this purpose, the musical instrument with the player is a good example. Just think about the long journeys that the players of the world have traveled with their instruments. What is more in the minds of the listeners is not a concept or his ideas, but the immortal name of that player.

Two main things should stand out to the listener about the new wave of your playing. First, it must be a powerful or noble idea never been heard before. Second, it should contain a message as well as comfort to the listener's heart or mind. If you manage to achieve these two things, then socializing with your new wave, will not be as onerous a task as one previously perceived. In the end, it will be labeled as a noble task. The listener is eager to turn their ears in anticipation of tones that they have never heard before and that will surely lift the creator. In the same way, as the essence of the message is close to the listener's mind, it will be grasped as if something that the listener has been looking for a long time has been found. The difference and the message are directly centered on human thought, and it is timely that the player first realizes it. Although many people plan very deeply in their minds, their plans lead to setbacks or delays in socializing such things. You must get rid of it.

Never, ever be satisfied with your creations and rest on them. You should always take steps to go beyond that. What can the listener think about you who created and popularize a new concept? Avoid breaking their trust as the listener has come to believe in you and that you can do much more than this. Therefore, you should seriously approach it. This process can be slow. There is nothing wrong with that. But for this, strong action is required. You must recognize it. Sacrifice is a must, and you must have a lot of patience for it. Artists are the ones who can easily address people's hearts. It is a good consolation for the player.

A great transformation cannot be expected without the performer imparting a meaningful message to society. You must give something to get something. Without that, no luck or other influences would ever happen. Many are anxiously waiting for that fortune to come. An unsown field will yield no harvest. It is also foolish to expect it will. The world is full of such people. Such a day will never come for them, and, tragically, they do not have the strength or wisdom to understand that their power or strength should be built through a well-managed process.

Characters like this carry the notion that nothing has ever failed me, and when it's too late or when they realize it, they don't have the technique or energy to remedy this wrong notion. Your mind is like a machine. Implementation of ideas will stall if it is not consistently put into practice. When a machine is not running it will become rusted and inactive. In the same way, human thought should flow continuously. Anyone representing the playing field not only should have a constant flow of creative energy but must also use it constantly. Every moment the concept of "I can and I must" is formed in one's mind, it will take the man to a higher level of energy. As such energy is possessed by any woman or man, it is only necessary to use a method to implement it.

Man must be aligned to turn opportunities into results. As in other fields, opportunities arise in the field of the player. It is an attempt by the player to downplay his role in not seeing such opportunities or trying to convince society by pretending that he hasn't seen such opportunities. He who is optimistic about it will make use of it and strengthen his journey. Those whose knowledge is scant and whose self-strength is lacking, let's such opportunities slip from their existence and prepare to move forward with time will never attain the position they strive to represent. Such opportunities are sometimes rare for them. Likewise, such an opportunity may never arise for such players.

Often one assesses one's various resources before preparing for a change or progression in one's playing. In the end, he contemplates a large stock of resources that he does not possess. Otherwise, a discussion will be made about it. By doing so, he undermines his inner self and leaves aside taking a new path or a step forward and remaining at the same level as they were. No great man in the world has had everything he wanted. They are constantly striving for that. With time, the player is unknowingly regressed from the playing field, and the player and his playing are also regressing. Take stock of your current resources frequently. After studying it well, you will understand what you have in the present is valuable for your future journey. It can only be realized after evaluating this and by a player who has a strong need to take a step forward. No one in any field of the world has ever heard of an opportunity where they got all the resources they wanted at once. All of them must be mastered step by step.

Every human being in the world should contribute to the growth and survival of his profession. The player is also a valuable character who should contribute to society. Therefore, you must present your contribution to the world. You should be prepared for that. In the end, it must be confirmed by the player. When the people represented in every field do their duty, the result is a meaningful world. You have chosen your field as a player. It should be that its representation contributes to the aforesaid strong existence. Whatever field you represent you should be satisfied. To achieve such satisfaction, the procedure should be identified and contributed to its socialization. The result is that you are involved in the process to take a step forward. For this, a new wave of playing is proposed. Then the aforesaid growth will happen within you.

Even if you don't know it, the assets and knowledge for this change or the new wave are stored inside you. You will understand it only when someone says it or compares it with an event in everyday society. It is futile to search for many things and to search far and wide in haste. After searching for that thing, you will realize that it has been contained in you for a long time. Therefore, there is no need to go far and worry. All this is embedded within you. No need to search around. Calmly ask your inner self first. Then your unique ideas will emerge. They are new ideas or concepts without any imitation. It is not surprising that when you gather from the society around you, they are all concepts copied from others. Don't make the mistake of taking things from others when you have a lot inside of you. Mind is a good investment when used properly. A correct and meaningful thought pattern is a guide that takes you in the direction you want.

Anyone with knowledge, method, and patience can change the shape and behavior of the external world. It has been so throughout history. It will happen to any player who is looking for a new wave of playing. Through that innovation, the existence of the player in the instrument and the entire universe will also change. Although the listener did not study about this, he also faced the same transformation without knowing it. Human beings will experience the development or improvement of the universe due to this change, which the entire human race contributes. For that reason, music will play a major role as it strongly affects the thinking pattern or mental development of man. Therefore, as the musician's contribution socializes a thought or an idea, he will add a meaningful message to the human heart which generates enjoyment and satisfaction. That will bring about change in the outside world.

About 80 to 85 percent of what a person thinks in a day or the thoughts that enter his mind is thoughts that have no value for him. If so, how much time a day does a man focused on unnecessary things? How valuable is the 10 to 15 percent included in that thinking? All those who strive to make this kind of change using it can make a huge and powerful change by directing the remaining 80 percent to meaningful thinking. Such thinkers are very rare in society. A majority is a large group of people who live with floating thoughts that cannot be translated into reality. If you spend your day with such unnecessary thoughts in your mind, you will not be able to highlight the strength of the vision and should adapt to a process which goes beyond that. Important thoughts get lost in the busy mind, and as a player, you are rarely busy. That is, dressing up for a stage performance, preparing for a live TV show, joining a conference, preparing for a recording, and making time for a music teaching job, to name a few. Among them, you should enter a quiet and lonely environment for your creations. Then you can approach your creation with a purified mind that is free of unwanted thoughts. You must build such an environment with effort. Your mind should be on a plane of serenity. You can't make a creation without inner calm, and the thoughts that arise in a chaotic atmosphere will slip away from you with that chaos. Therefore, the knowledge and methodology of a calm mind emerge strongly, and it is the only foundation of creativity. It will happen with or without knowledge.

You must have something powerful within yourself that you can express to make a difference in people. You play the role of a player in a world full of players. You weren't the only player there. Therefore, you must actively take the role of a meaningful player among the ordinary.

You will always love to associate with or join a group of people who appreciate the new wave of your playing. They are probably always with you. But what is needed is to double or triple that number of listeners. You must acquire a new group of followers. You should make a systematic effort for that. Many people must flock to the new wave of music. You must spend a long time on that and nobody in the music industry can do it in a day or two. At one time the listener will have difficulty understanding the new trend and after listening to a few such pieces he will gradually come to enjoy it and come closer to the new wave and embrace it. Because the listener has minimal understanding of your music or styles, only a few insightful listeners may understand your music. But the majority may not understand it as they are not serious listeners. You will be a failure in developing a new wave if you always try to give what listeners ask. You must establish your opinion in them and incline them towards it. Not all listeners in the world can be satisfied with your new wave. Don't even try it. Striving for that task is a failed effort. Because there are people in society who do not care about other people's opinions, who think that their identity will be destroyed by respecting them, who think that they are on a higher level than others, and this group will never turn into such a new wave. There are times when they publicly criticize others when they do what they cannot do. You must keep moving forward and remember that these criticisms are not eternal. As your audience grows, such criticisms will fade away. What is required is your continuous effort.

You naturally build a great relationship with the listener through your creations. That listener may not have met or seen you. Your personal information may not be known by them. Sometimes they may like to associate or see you, but that is difficult to accomplish for every listener. Your listener may be in a faraway foreign land. But based on the strength of your playing or your new wave, he can become a very close and powerful fan without even knowing you. Even if you don't get a chance to meet them or recognize them, that listener will never leave you. This is an asset for a player, it makes your journey easier, and your steps are firm.

In addition to all the knowledge that you have in trying to popularize a change in playing, the thought about the creation of the new wave must be strongly embedded in your mind for a long time. Then this mental activity, including the knowledge you have and the physical resources, will motivate you well for that creation. The thoughts that form in your mind are more powerful than anything else. So be careful to build that trust. Your idea and concept will then not only be successful, but it will also acquire you good practice. By practice, many things can be launched correctly and successfully, and thus you unconsciously join the process of training your mind for this creation and by doing it continuously you will become an expert in it.

Few people have overcome their physical exertion and advanced in life. That opinion has led to an ideology in the world today. The strength of that thought makes the creative process a reality. Right thinking was the main reason for the success of many people who conquered the world. That thinking has led them to those achievements. Activities of them also happened with that thinking. This is the kind of thinking you're unconsciously looking for in your new wave of playing. This powerful thought keeps your hands working properly every time you pick up the instrument you have mastered. Every moment the thought and the process of the hands are balanced, the sound or style you desire will emerge. No one can stop it from being a new wave.

It is not an easy task for one person or organization to change a musical instrument or a style of music by force or effort. One's effort for that is also a failed effort. The damage caused to the field by such an effort is also immense. Millions and billions of fans are still listening to songs and pieces very popular during the Renaissance, Baroque, Classical and Romantic periods and in the 60s and 70s. It is no secret that these songs and pieces are widely used and sold in the world even today. If such old things are removed from the field, many people who depend on them will be abandoned. Likewise, the commitment made by the music industry to bring it to the present state will be in vain. So, shouldn't justice be done for that? Therefore, what should be done for that is not to remove the trunk or the root of a tree? If you do, the world knows very well what will happen, when you create a new wave with a difference and in a matching and pleasing way other music lovers will gradually join hands with you with the new wave of your playing. It will happen slowly and the damage to other genres or playing style will be very small. Millions and billions of fans will not become one's new wave overnight.

METHODOLOGY AND APPROACH

for the New Wave

Chapter 4

"You don't seem to know Illusion.
That is why you are still in the Illusion".

A common question often asked by young amateur players is 'why my playing is not popular?' He does not see several problems in it, and all those problems should be explored respectively. Your knowledge and skills alone cannot achieve dominance in a field. One's thinking should be spread over a wide range of different aspects. You will have the opportunity to see concepts and use them wisely. When you are ready, you will have many such successes. You should do such things yourself [creating a new wave] it is not appropriate to expect such things from others. You, the observant, may experience that you perceive things that many others do not. You should have a strong commitment to this. You must be active regardless of the time you must have for this, your goal in being a player in a new wave, and you will not feel tired because of the pleasantness of it. There must be actions. Without actions or activities, you are nowhere. With these movements sometimes there may be failures. Failures teach you invaluable things. It's a must for a long and successful journey in your music career. Thinking and dreaming only will not take you to your destination. There must be 'Actions'.

Start creating. Your knowledge must combine with your willpower. Creativity needs a powerful aim. In the beginning, you may hesitate, get delayed, and play some wrong notes. This is very common. An infant never starts walking as soon as he is born. You will gradually improve with experience and time. Time will settle more things if you are patient and full of purpose. Dreaming won't take you to success. You must work hard to get it.

Your desire or powerful aim to be a player with a new trend won't get you success in a hurry. It takes time. So, calm down. You must be active throughout the day with your activities and don't try to expect anything from luck or miracles. Between every activity, there must be a pause or time to go into the heart of your fans or audience. Always people think about themselves. He is the most important person in this whole world and your message or whatever the activity must go beyond that and then only you will be able to get their attention. For this, your message must contain something new or something with a new wave.

Ability is one factor. Popularity is another factor. Abilities will be well-proven when very talented players are seen in unpopular fields. They are limited to a small area in this busy world. Similarly, it is not surprising that some players with limited abilities are very popular in the industry. It doesn't usually happen by luck. Opportunities often arise for anyone with talents, knowledge of the gaps in the present market, and the way to combine such things. The same is true in the music industry. Society decides whether such situations happen because of luck. Luck aside you must seek what is that you're looking for in the music industry and what you'll build up as you stay in the industry for a long time. You can't learn that just by following other players. You need to be constantly on the lookout for management, the current market, new concepts, subtle paths forward, and aspects that others may not see. The courage to go forward is another factor in any field with your abilities. Other people's motivations or trajectories may present themselves. Together with all that, your goals must be met then a certain foundation will be built by gathering the events for the development or existence of music from many societies. For this, you must, as said before, never let your goals get blurred. One must put in a lot of effort to become a player who must achieve fame in the instrument. He must have the strength to endure continuously and can never reach that level without hard work.

Any man can learn art and skill, but he must understand well how to use that art and skill in the world. Your behavior is determined by using that art and skill and recognizing its value in using it with proper management for your tasks. Your character is directly determined using that art and skill, and it is yours to recognize its value in trying to use it with proper management of recognition. Your cooperation with other players and helping them and supporting them in their valuable tasks also must concede is a vital path in your journey. Don't try to fulfill your journey alone. It's not an easy task. By giving you gain something. There must be a pleasing strong link in your industry for your and others' survival. Therefore, you must get rid of Jealousy, anger, disturbance, and cheating. If you are not well aligned, then you will be left alone with what you have learned. The world will need your skills and using them will build your identity. Everyone has different and new methods and actions which is uncommon. In those uncommon abilities, there is a new wave that you expect. This is your identity, follow that.

From school age, one builds goals in his life and studies the actions to be taken to maintain his existence no matter what his goals are. In his mind, various new concepts and methods that no one else has used before are gradually formed. Often these new concepts or methods are rare in the world. It is natural to feel different because as said before, you are a special person, different from others in the world, a very different person, full of qualities that others do not have. No need to imitate others or copy from any other method. Therefore, your ability difference is in your thinking or what you are looking for. You must use the difference for your survival, and then it is inevitable to create a change or a new wave in you. When you enter society, you can go far. You have something that others haven't used, unseen, powerful, and by using it you will build a new wave in any field.

You must first study what you need to do to create any change or wave in the playing and you must have a proper understanding of it. The most essential thing here is the time you spend with your instrument. The time you spend with an instrument is the result of your playing. It is a fine investment. The more you develop a relationship with that instrument, the easier it will be for you. Therefore, the first thing to do is to master this musical instrument in your hand. Without such a set of experiences, it is difficult for you to take a step forward. Preparation is very important before we face an exam. By staying in any profession for many years, that person will become a strong person with a set of experiences in that field. Experienced doctor can cure diseases successfully. Fewer mistakes are made by an experienced driver. Going to an experienced teacher is a very sound investment. An experienced actor is the soul of a role. Similarly, an experienced player entertains the listener with a different, meaningful and new powerful message. Just check a popular piece of music that always contains a difference, from other creations. Therefore, first, you should check your connection with your musical instrument not once but many times before entering this work.

The second step is that the wider your knowledge of music, the easier this task will be for you. It is not a uniform method, but a thorough exploration of the patterns from different angles, even if you don't like them. With this effort, you will move past the conflicting opinions of certain musical patterns or styles, as well as depth, meaning, color, rhythm, and harmony, to the steps that will lift you to a higher level.

You are a visionary for a new wave of creation. Therefore, a good understanding and study of the theory of music are mandatory for quality, correct, and meaningful composition. That is your third step. Albert Einstein (1879-1955) pointed out that about eighty percent of what we learn in school during our school age is not useful for us when we integrate with society. However, underestimating or ignoring these principles will not make your composition harmonize. The theories in music you learn in the school will be useful for a better creation. Therefore, the manipulation or control of the musical instrument and the confirmation of the theoretical standard is an art. Naturally, artistry emerges from each process when it is deeply used and strongly invested in any field. It becomes a skill in you and invests in that art well and practice. Not just a skill but by absorbing it in practice, you get many chances and opportunities. When the theories of music and the knowledge of your musical instrument that you have acquired over the years are combined, the right creation emerges, and to create a new wave in it, acquiring a good understanding of the current musical patterns or styles is the third deep task. Keep in mind that all three of these factors will be strongly built up as the foundation of your new wave. Therefore, it is very important that you are always aware of these three principles.

There is a famous saying that "It is better to play something that is technically poor but touches the heart, than something which is technically perfect and touched nothing". It depends on how you arrange your creation.

The human brain is divided into two parts, the left brain, and the right brain. Keep in mind that the right brain-controlled technical knowledge, thinking power, and emotions (anger, and sadness) are very important for your new wave. First, the technical knowledge contained in this should be highlighted. Secondly, in manipulating the thought pattern, a balance will be maintained. Likewise, emotions will determine how these two tasks will be managed or become a reality. The more successful the third factor, the more it will determine socialization. Its strength will determine success or failure. It is the most important thing to emerge first, in that creation that reveals its content and taste. Because you create for listeners. Capturing him is the first and most important task. In this way, a new experience that has not been heard or felt before is created in him by this creation, and its evaluation is based on the effort you take to introduce this listener to a new world using feeling or taste.

But some neuroscientists recently stated that creativity does not involve a single brain region or single side of the brain. Anyhow you are born to create. Without creation as a player, you are nowhere.

You will question yourself if you are the perfect person with such a set of abilities for your creativity. Remember that the weakness you build yourself up mentally will place you on a very sad level. Be very careful not to try to hold anything in your mind but "I can do it". As soon as the meaning of defeat or negation is implanted in the subconscious mind, that thought is sure to strongly paralyze your existence and instincts and sometimes dull your abilities. You are perfect with abilities and innate talents. Naturally, examples of this are very visible within you. Most of the time, when choosing a new dress, the first thing you do when you enter the store is to check whether the color of the dress matches your body color. Similarly, the design of the garment (multiple stripes or squares, or color combination) will be thought of twice. Standing in front of the mirror in the store, the garment will be placed on your body and will be viewed once or twice in different directions. But only if the dress fits, do you go to the room reserved for it in the shop to check whether the dress is right or wrong or if it fits your body size. Furniture placed in certain places in your home or a flowering plant planted in a pot will be placed in the most suitable place in the house and should be looked from different viewpoints. If unsatisfied, come back and adjust the item slightly and set it aside. Evaluating in this way will eventually lead to the decision that the pot is suitable for the place. See, in both examples, isn't that creative potential within you that you haven't realized yet contained in it? This is a useful little example. In the same way, when you use those adjustments successfully in preparing your hair, especially in applying certain colors to beautify the face of women, in choosing a pair of shoes that match the dress, it emerges that the understanding and ability to adapt or create something new in you has been well highlighted.

Now you don't need rehearsal to be creative. It is time to get ready for a start. Experience the beauty of nature that you often encounter. Experience it a little or study its existence thoroughly. Memorize its location. In that experience, its location or the space, shape, and color of the foliage and environment conveys something meaningful and is perfected with a wonderful message that evokes your imagination and artistic sensibilities. Remember this is the beginning of creation. The journey through it is very powerful.

If someone who is made aware of all this takes their instrument and tries to create and cannot bring out something meaningful or satisfying from it, then the obstacle is within you. Because again, as mentioned at the beginning of this chapter, a lack of complete understanding of the musical instrument being used or studied, a lack of proper understanding of the theories of music, and a lack of deep and meaningful study of music is the gap. If so, refer to those fundamentals. There is plenty of time. Avoid building a fear about it. According to a well-known psychologist Joseph Murphy, if a man does not excel, he becomes a legend between the ages of 60-90. Don't be afraid of time. If you die without being strong, it will surely cause fear on that day. Likewise, preparing for such a long journey in the middle of life is not at all impossible.

Surveys have shown if 100 dying people (men and women) are asked, what would you do differently if you could be born again as a child? Ninety-seven percent said, "Oh, how good if I don't miss out again, I will remove all my mistakes and become a strong character". Three percent said, "I, did, the best I can and I left something for posterity, and I must leave my life to make that opportunity for them". At the end of your life, build a character of such a meaningful and great person and leave this world. Become a character that can make such a statement and enter a meaningful farewell from this world.

Even in an age where the world is more competitive and complex than any other era, the resources, knowledge, and technology you can acquire for a new existence are everywhere you look. Therefore, the knowledge that surpasses the competition and the resources that the world has given you to move forward are immense. Therefore, you have no grounds for excuses. You must build up your dream on the foundation you have built.

That's what every player should learn on their journey to find a new wave of playing. Be it a study of the core and avoid going beyond that. Succeed in the task of understanding it. Build your identity on those understandings.

In the same way, by studying the ability or actions of other strong people, you cannot acquire strength by praising them. Competitiveness should be established in your mind. Remember thoroughly, that the competition that builds up in the mind must always be only with you. It is a competition aimed at your progress. Don't try to be better than anyone or number one. Always try to be a player better than yesterday. The core of that competitiveness will be broken every moment when competition with others is built. Few other characters in the world are like you who are chasing a new wave of thinking from a different angle than others with different abilities. It should be understood thoroughly and if the facts are such, it is tragic as well as unreasonable for such a character to build competition with others. Realize that your opponent is always within you. How to build competition with yourself? Every night before going to sleep, remember the important tasks (important for your future) that need to be done tomorrow. If it is confusing, take a piece of paper and write them down with numbers in order. The most important tasks should be at the forefront and should be marked number one. Wake up early to make the day meaningful and get important tasks done. Be anxious to implement those important tasks one by one. If for some reason you are not able to accomplish any task that you had planned, try to plan it again that night to accomplish it or succeed in it. Thus, the failure of some important tasks to reap successful results and the reason contained in it is a sharp victory you get for the success of life by applying your studies, as well as an excellent investment built for one's existence. Through this kind of investment, the players understand their existence well, and by implementing some plans, a good understanding and a meaningful set of experiences will be built in themselves, and through it, such breakdowns and defeats will not happen in the future. Imagine each day that a kind, gentle and hopeful day has dawned. Then only such a set of emotions will flow to you. The day will be exciting, and the aspirant will get many fruits. Bring only competent, authentic concepts to the community. Always stay away from evil and abusive concepts. Keep in mind that when such ideas are born in the mind, the creation fails. Because the understanding, emphasis, and thinking power of the man's technical knowledge space is controlled by the right brain, the anger generated with the emergence of these evil, violent ideas in the mind, emerges beyond all these feelings and abilities, and thus all the creative energy of a musician, player or a person representing any field, will be lost. Anger, sad feelings and taste are generated in the right brain sometimes the mind is not able to balance several opposing emotions. Therefore, it is extremely important to first understand your course and identify the damage that could happen. Then you will be able to realize a lot. It will plan to take a step forward. This will make you powerful in ways you never imagined.

Creation will never end if the world exists. There is no time or date for birth. What has happened is that it was temporarily omitted in the middle. You must strongly reject all those who hold the opinion that it cannot be done. Likewise, it is tragic that they remain in the field saying that something cannot be done. Their influence or damage in any field is immense. Its strongest impact is on the few who struggle to survive in the right way. But the experts avoid these things and keep their journey well aligned. Study the action of these characters whenever you get a chance. Along with the change in their existence comes a great change in their lives. Rather than stagnating on results, such people are enthusiastic about different plans, and ultimately experience strong success due to that new wave or change. Success is getting what you want using a process.

Look at your playing career in a broader way than you are today. Or try to experience it. Build strong confidence in yourself. Never allow it to be broken or damaged. Nothing is impossible with such strong faith. Any force that opposes you will be blown away like dust blown by a strong wind.

Believe that I can, in every moment possible. Remove any failures and defeats from your mind and thoughts as soon as possible. In the end, experience the feeling of 'I can'. Place your feet on such a strong foundation. The satisfaction of its step-by-step journey will be the change or new wave you wish for.

You may have been a stubborn student who didn't care about your studies during your time at school or a disobedient student who sat in the last row of the class. Due to your certain opinions and ideas in that era, you may be a student who engaged in activities away from the teachers and students in the class. Such students are a common sight in any school. They also associate with the same group in school. This situation is common in any school in the world. But if you do thorough research on them, one will understand that the students who are at the level of this kind of stubborn and quarrelsome are a group of very talented people. It has been revealed that most of the students, who have not received the love and kindness of their parents, or who have no parents or otherwise are victims of some breakdowns or mental pressures in their family system, often end up in this situation. Most of these students often transform into completely different characters when they enter society after their schooling is interrupted. As they enter society, their previously mentioned strong abilities are put into action over time, which challenges their isolation or their marginalization in society. By harnessing the powerful abilities inherent in them during this awakening, they achieve a great transformation in their lives. They work above the people who were at a very high level in the class and often the projects and businesses started by these people end up being worked by people from the group they studied strongly in school. With this message, if you were such a character during your school days, this example will surely be a great effort towards your difference or strength. No one in the world can be called weak people. It is criminal for society to label people as weak in this way. If so, you are the right person for a change or wave in their playing career. The defeats and breakdowns we experienced in the past tell us a deep message. Build your foundation on that message. Even if that foundation is not pleasant to you, it is a solid foundation.

As mentioned earlier in this chapter, you need to have a light mind for composing. Attempting to perform the task with an unbalanced or confused mind will fail. Although the experiences or lessons we can gain from a troubled, complex, or chaotic mind are important. However, in creation, you must approach the task alone with a calm mind. Therefore, get used to experiencing solitude. The leaders in certain fields like to isolate themselves from the complex society once every two weeks or even once a month. In that solitude you can identify many messages that are deep and meaningful, colored by your thought pattern and reflections which are very meaningful for your creation.

Through a good vision, you can enter the desired plane or foundation. But you must have a proper plan to achieve that level. The use of planning is the highest level of management. Therefore, the player should always work with a good understanding of this, and it is important to be concerned in every task to maintain the quality of the plan at a high level. The plans used in the journey to make the journey of the player successful are the crucial and decisive moments of his journey. For example, if he intends to release his music to a world-renowned music platform, he should carefully study when is the appropriate time, the positive value of the music pieces included in the recording, the advertising method used for the sale, the age group targeted, etc. There must be a plan. Based on the above, you will acquire the desired sales and publicity for your music and creations. Any player looking for a new wave can't be satisfied with a few of these performances and creations, because creations have no end. There is only a beginning. A few years after the release of the first composition, any player will not be satisfied with that first performance. It must be so for the sake of progress in playing. Again, prepare yourself for your second presentation. In this way, you will surely align the development of your playing career with a new wave.

In many players pursuing a new wave of playing, there are certain differences (intellectually or thinking) from existence to perfectionists, and unconsciously to them, those transformations have been maintained since childhood. No matter what field they represent, they are rallying to demonstrate this difference. In the same way, for the betterment of mankind or the world, it is a precious task for man to submit to such influences or establish himself. It should be so. Therefore, the transformation of this player to a change in someone or a new wave of a player is very meaningful for the survival and value of the player's performance. It can be clearly understood if we look at these players. They are very quiet, and graceful, and love a quiet environment. They have very few friends. (Many people in busy fields have very few friends because they are so busy, that they can't make time for friends.) Without active listening, there is little they talk about. They have mastered one of the most difficult tasks in the world: listening. One can acquire many things by listening. It is a valuable resource for a player looking for a new wave of playing. You must think to express yourself. Then it is easy to imagine what meaning your thinking will take. But listening has been cited as one of the most important tasks in the world. Understanding it is also an easy task. It is a valuable study in one's life as one constantly gets to absorb ideas or concepts while listening. Reading makes you a real human being and listening also is a great investment. It is a precious gift that one often receives, usually for free. How valuable is that gift? (Not about the gossip that is used more in society) These values should be gathered for the new wave of the player or the change he is pursuing. Where new concepts are lost, new ideas do not emerge, and where new concepts are gathered, the possibility of new ideas emerging is immense. As well as listening like this, it is extremely important to see many things very carefully. The player should not just see the struggle, the sweet beauty, sorrow, or the pleasure. This kind of thing comes naturally from a musical instrument. Try to see as much space and form as possible. Immerse yourself deeply in these two things to have a better understanding of how to incorporate your ideas into this space and form. Space surrounds us and form must be recognized. It must be learned to use it to properly establish the form in the spaces. By recognizing the forms, a performer sees and adapting to those forms, value is naturally added to your creation. The composer (performer) who recognizes space and form naturally controls his listener. (It's like fitting the furniture into an empty room.) Just like the world's great authors, scientists, explorers, and philosophers have grasped a large society, players also grasp the listeners with an unheard-of concept through a new wave of creation.

All those who have a desire or love for strength will often have opportunities to launch that strength. It means "the seeker finds" in its nature. In such a situation, never leave that little chance. Because a little bit of one's progress is polished indication that you are stepping into the foundation of success in the task you are striving to launch. The accumulation of such trifles will form a powerful path. When an arrow is released from the bow, it finds its target and never returns. Once time has passed, time will never come back to you. Once a word is spoken, whether it is right or wrong, it cannot be changed again. In the same way, do not let the small opportunity that you get slip away and reap the rewards of it because that opportunity will probably never come again. Such opportunities are rarely missed by a man who has a strong plan for a journey in his mind. He will acquire the natural sense as they are always awake looking for such things.

In the journey you have launched, the naysayers will possibly join you. They may be a close friend of yours or a relative, or maybe a respected character. Avoid listening to them in the first place. Avoid them as much as possible or withdraw from the company. Because every time they see someone else in society implementing many meaningful things that they cannot do, they are confused, and they are often anxious to build opposition to it. Those of you who are looking for a new facet or new wave of playing should avoid them and never, ever listen to them. Look at their lives when you get a chance. In a common society where many people gather every day very slowly, a group of people who are in a sad state and live their lives with common old ideas will be visible. As a player who is ready to line up for a new wave or a player who has started that journey, do not allow yourself to be overwhelmed by such childish characters.

For the sake of intellectual growth, you should regularly line up and be eager to read books containing much data about it and try out the research or predictions in it. Then you will have a clear understanding and a plan that will turn your journey into a powerful action that will lift you to a crowd that has said no to you. As ideas and concepts become integrated into our thinking, transformations will line up before us to the point of trying to make choices like never before. Such ideas, concepts, or thoughts direct your course in various meaningful directions and contain the foundation or existence that one aspires to.

In the journey you launched as a player, you will have to face various obstacles, mental breakdowns, unrealistic criticisms, and unexpected transformations. You must build powerful strength to face every such event. That is the strength of your playing. If you have reached such a footing as a performer, do not be afraid of any force, mental breakdown, or naysayers. Don't divert from your journey. Because all these things will be broken by the strength of yours playing. Every moment you lift it up and never get hurt or let down by it. There are also cases where some musicians are marginalized in the field due to such unfortunate influences or tragically declining in the field. Check carefully and it will be confirmed that these people lack the strength or proper investment in that field. So, no one who is well established should have any doubt about it. Even though it is a group of people who lack proper strength, who always shakes or breaks down, the strong man does not get caught by any such failed plan or natural influence. Strength comes as a result of a long journey. An extraordinary character can go to such lengths and such characters are common in society. Therefore, there is a great and priceless value in every such rare thing.

It is a common thing in society that people who do not understand such a journey and who do not have the strength to launch such a journey themselves make very rude and harsh criticisms, obstacles, and complaints towards people who are outstanding in their field or who are engaged in a meaningful journey. Although this used to abundant in the past, there are few such people in society today. Their actions are not strong enough to launch an attack for a player who is stable in any field. But since there is nothing, they can do, they will spend their time and effort on such unnecessary and stressful things, and they will spend their lives in stress. Do not be afraid of such people. The hindrances they make to your progress are only temporary.

The natural energy that you must possess is before you, and within you. All you must do is access it. Don't feel alone or defeated. We own the world around us. It is the right thing to be done by man. By using natural energy, one can rise to greatness. It is unfortunate to oppose it or turn your back on it. Many people add such unfortunate moments to their existence and the wise will reap the benefits of planning well for their existence. That fruit is for the entire human race.

To achieving this, here are ten steps you should follow.

1. Be able to make decisions according to your opinion.

2. Reject other people's opinions.
3. Never lose heart from your strongly built purpose.
4. Never let a thought of defeat enter your mind.
5. Always keep your inner self happy.
6. Be honest with yourself and society.
7. Stay away from incompatible people as much as possible.
8. Step towards the goal without doubt or fear.
9. Go one or two steps further than the distance you to go.
10. Avoid criticizing others.

Having formed such determinations, you will surely achieve a new path.

You must make the effort to launch all this. The connection and knowledge you have with your musical instrument, the knowledge of the theory of music, the understanding of one's subject or its various aspects of styles, the personal experiences of the player in society, all these things will help you greatly in building this new wave and launching it. The task, or the socialization of your personal experiences during your lifetime, must be done by yourself. All other values and processes only help you to reach such a level. It is the nature of human existence that when one is mentally and physically aligned for a purpose and goal, all his or her senses, thoughts, and every gesture are prepared for that desired task. Study carefully, about some of the stalwarts around you in any field. All these people have the above-mentioned qualities and they have continuously occupied the desired position or plane because they have built strong goals and built strong aims until victory is achieved. Everyone who has started such a journey using such thoughts and methods will be able to identify the obstacles in front of them and they will easily use the remedies for those obstacles. All that is required is to enter that plane. You should wake up from a half-sleep and recognize the reality in the world. Like a fast-tracking arrow shot from the bow, one must aim precisely at a target. Obstacles before anyone with such goals and objectives will be broken and shattered like pottery. Thoughts are so powerful. Childish thoughts can lead you to a very sad or defeated world, while meaningful and powerful thoughts can lift you to a pinnacle of great determination. What should be done is to understand now how to end the journey successfully. There is no end to that journey. Don't be anxious to hear an end but continue that journey. After you and behind you is a huge group of organized men who is there in every corner of the world to continue your task. The strength is in abundance. It is sad that man blindly stays idle in it. One should enter that space with an open mind with an understanding. Then the world waiting to be entered will be visible to him. That dawning world is not just for you but for the sake of all mankind.

Leave the illusion forever. It is a hollow bubble that contains nothing inside it. The player's action is the result of a chain of decisive thoughts connected with reality. It is a message suitable for the spiritual or fast-paced society today, which has transcended its new wave and moved the human mind in a strong and meaningful direction by listening to socializing new concepts and transcending conservative habits. The modern trend should be socialized by the player for the betterment of society, with the idea of uplifting the industry.

Get rid of mythical forces forever. It is a dark membrane embraced in the minds of weak minds. Build a strong mindset that aligns with your goals and objectives.

There are three main steps one should follow to become a strong player.

1. Identification of proper technique.
2. Mastering the craft with meaningful management and control.
3. Winning the stage.

To the extent that one is encased in a framework of occult forces or illusions to becoming a player without the above three points, the player is not recognized for his true potential or appropriate reality. Success is often not a result of some unseen force. Through such unseen forces, to what extent does the ability to control or bind the listener emerges?

Such invisible failing forces will not hold you up, and such beliefs will hinder your natural abilities. As mentioned earlier, you are suffering from a belief built on unseen forces that suppress your abilities.

World-famous British poet John Milton (1608-1674) went blind. But he was a powerful poet. America's 32nd President Franklin D. Roosevelt (1882-1945) sat in a wheelchair and ruled America for 12 years very successfully. Although the world-renowned German musician Ludwig Van Beethoven (1770-1827) became deaf at the age of 28, in the remaining 29 years he composed many unique compositions. All their success was not achieved by any force. They were achieved only by using practice, knowledge, and intuition.

By practicing, the skills or habits are established in one, and using knowledge mastery of the subject takes place. Intelligence controls all this and is its power. The power of intelligence will manifest itself through its proper management. Therefore, a player should possess the first two of these three powerful elements over time and dedicate himself to acquiring that level for the sake of intellectual development. No matter how technically strong or experienced you are, if you are not intelligent, you will not only create confusing situations. You will face many such disputes and turbulent moments in your life journey. One can often achieve intelligence through learning and reading and there is nothing that cannot be done by reaping the proper fruits from it. Therefore, you have all the necessary qualifications to align yourself to enter a new wave using the system. Time flies so fast that you don't know how much time there is, and you must move at the same speed. It is often a failure of character to claim that time is running out for one's accomplishments. Such a statement is not heard from one who has learned the power of preparation and has a firm grasp of this. Power of preparation is determined by time management and one understands of meaningful processes. It is natural to lose a great deal of time and lose control of one's subject upon entering a field to which one is not suited for the role of a player. Thus, by allowing oneself to lose one's resources or existence, one becomes defeated and deeply disappointed, and in the end, that delay will never be able to rise again to victory or reality.

One can say that the whole world is an illusion just like the present moment. You will meet such people in society. Just thinking a little bit about this will make you realize that this is not true. Whoever endorses the first opinion will eventually get a backlash. Such characters are common. Such statements are only a temporary elevation of the said person and when the unique characters of the world are studied its falsities will be well understood.

The small things that you miss are useful for some development or growth in existence, while those subtle things can affect a breakdown or setback. Therefore, you should focus your attention on such subtle things and you should be very careful about the actions you take in your future journey. Restoring or establishing things that has been missed by you, will be an uphill task. Therefore, every moment you take a step forward in making decisions, you should think wisely, and the purpose of your journey will directly affect this. Even if you are agitated on the outside, you should be very calm on the inside. A calm mind sees many things correctly and choosing the right things will build up energy. The player is a character who is built on human relations among people and should not only direct the listener in a certain direction but also open new paths. Therefore, it is difficult to make huge changes at once in the way that a player can accomplish the task with such subtle things, and the listener will not have the opportunity to identify such changes. It is a gradual process. Based on these small changes, the work will gradually align with time. Progress goes with progress and a breakdown will be followed by a setback with such breakdowns.

If you have good discipline and self-control your decision-making will likely be correct on most occasions. Therefore, many people who do not respect discipline in such situations will fail in their decisions and their journey will also be hampered as a result of their poor decision making. Discipline is well-established in gifted people and Intelligence is power. Geniuses uses that power properly with proper investment. There is no other force in human control that can compare with that power. Intelligence makes us see many things that are invisible to the naked eye and makes many unheard things heard. (This is very important for an accomplished player.) Not only will the previously mentioned discipline be mastered, but many of these will be required for survival. The message of every religion in the world is about righteous living. If the whole world practices this, the world will be very peaceful and beautiful. However, despite having strong faith in that religion, very few people have adapted to live according to it. When a man possesses intelligence, his action becomes rational. Hence, he will manage his existence, advance new concepts and handle human relations well. You will be able to see almost anything. Therefore, the origin of philosophy is intelligence.

Before going to bed every night, spend some time in bed thinking about all your top tasks that need to be done tomorrow. Give priority to your efforts to establish a new wave in the playing. Let your subconscious mind hear the style, tone, and rhythm it contains. Most of what anyone thinks before going to sleep at night captures his powerful subconscious mind and those thoughts will be strongly embedded in your mind during night sleep. After you wake up in the morning, it will be a powerful force, channel this into action or to a creation you do with your instruments. When you go to sleep negative or worrying over the day's tragic defeats, a very different outcome occurs. You are bound to have a day of defeat. Reflect on positive things every day before sleep. Therefore, spend a few moments before going to bed thinking about the important tasks that need to be launched tomorrow. Even if you are half-asleep like this, even if you go into a deep sleep, whatever the first thought is, it will be firmly embedded in the subconscious mind. It will greatly affect your life activities.

These are the core techniques that have been researched and tested in the world to build a strong and great life. Its success has also been confirmed. Many great people in the world use those methods and have achieved unimaginable levels of success by using their own experiences as well as the modern techniques. You too have every right to try such opportunities. You have the right to represent yourself in whatever field you admire or aspire to be an expert in that field. First, identify those core and meaningful techniques. Second, put it to use. Strength emerges in recognition and practice. Then you will have your rights. That is the goal you hope for. These techniques should not be taken as buying goods and services from a market. All you must do is put these things in your mind and put them to good use. For this, you must wake up. You who are awakened must be wise. Only the intellect will see these techniques.

I didn't write anything to read
There is nothing colorful to see
It is futile to seek smoothness
You listen and stop
Your steps also became still
Be it love, lust, or beauty
Pleasure or sorrow

That thought which
I try to convey
Is not my effort
It's the message of
My Guitar.

SOCIALIZATION OF THE NEW WAVE

Chapter 5

"Your instrument has little to say to you. But it has a lot to say to others".

Once you get into the new wave of your playing, you don't have to worry about socializing it. Today the entire universe is a market. You have entered an era where there are many ways to sell something or spread the new trend of your music. Likewise, you should make sure that these tasks are not a challenge for you. Therefore, you should not worry. Because you live in a world where there is a variety of music of different shapes and styles. Its strongest and most important function is to try to socialize with the new wave of your playing at a time when the world is always really expecting every service or product for its name or a new set of emotions, a new meaning for its existence. This is a valuable transaction between you and the listener. Relationships are a developing process. A series of events will lift you to progress in your playing career. This should be the goal of your playing career.

No matter what instrument you play, you must navigate every nook and cranny of this global village. For that, the world has shaped as said before and is ready to lift you for this work. Today, in an age where newspapers and television are losing its demand to social media, the challenge you have is quite relaxed. Start small and slow. This is not a suggestion that will bring you comfort.

This is just as important as starting something big, it is time to start small and start planning. It is the right practice for you. First, connect on very popular Facebook with some musicians who you think will be useful in their playing career. Build a deeper relationship with them over time. Through this, you can slowly start spreading your message in the country where you live. (Remember that this campaign you run does not cost anything).

If the new wave launch by you fails, it will inevitably be your failure or delay. If you do not overcome any obstacle, the battle involved will lead you to a defeat. This will prove that you will leave the fight without even realizing it. Each mission creates a fierce battle. You must conquer it on your own. Because in the middle of the journey, there are many things you can learn, actions that can change the course, new concepts are born, and the damage caused by stopping in the middle without finishing the journey is enormous. Don't think of failures as obstacles. Those are invaluable lessons. A perfect journey can only be managed like this. No one likes to accept defeat. Throughout history only victories become reality. These victories must be bold and meaningful. If such hardness and meaning are not in that activity, it won't last and not be everlasting. Therefore, it will become a victory only when sharp competition is built into one.

Especially for the popularity of a beginner's playing, the support from society is very little. Sometimes, one rarely receives publicity or financial support, and it should be mentioned that it continues very rarely. The environment and society and its contributions develop strong expectations and it is a process that should build competition and toughness in you. The concept of society and the environment and strongly expecting its contribution is a wise action; building competition and toughness in you is necessary. You should first understand the reality of any profession in the world as well as how the player is represented. Likewise, in the performance of a soloist, you are alone in its inherent nature.

Socializing a new message is a much easier task for a well-known, experienced, and connected strong player. As soon as he makes a composition, it enters society, and the listeners grasp it or fall in love with that creation. A skilled archer rarely misses the target. No matter how sharp and strong the arrow in his hand is, he must have a powerful bow to use it otherwise. Likewise, it is not surprising that an experienced archer with such a sharp arrow would not have a similarly powerful bow nearby. Even if it takes some time to build this relationship, you must build it with time and you must have a lot of patience and management for it. Explore some of the latest creations from the internet (YouTube). You will understand it well then. Keep in mind that they, like you are players who started very slowly.

You have to include music lovers who have as much understanding of your playing style as possible in your designed Facebook profile and include professional musicians, singers, music students, music recording or editing technicians, music critics, music teachers, conductors, writers, or reviewers. Always try your best to advertise only your music and your activities. Try your best to visualize your image as a player. Only market yourself and your music. Facebook profiles that are made up of discourses about politics, sports, business, or other subjects are not effective for the tasks you expect because your field is music. Likewise, you are a player. So first understand who you are and how your path should be shaped. Truly your Facebook profile should be a paradise full of artists. Whatever instrument you master, add as many players as possible to your list of friends who study that instrument as their main instrument. Avoid linking to your Facebook account for the sake of pleasing certain people. Include only the people you need to build your image.

Make a short and light creation once or twice a month and post it on your Facebook profile. (1 minute or about 1 1/2 minutes). It must contain a little or a hint of your new wave. For this first creation, you will surely get both positive and negative reactions. Avoid thinking too deeply about these responses. Most of the reviews are unjustified reviews and well-versed and professional music reviewers don't have the time to spend on the work of an artist like you. Therefore, keep in mind that 50% of the reviews that come to you at the beginning are substandard reviews. Do not change yourself just from the influence of society. You must change society. Therefore, you are not encouraged to pay special attention to these reviews. Accurate and properly standardized criticism is very rare in the world. Such critics are rare among the common people of society. Criticism is powerful research that determines the merits and demerits of a work of art after a well-studied analysis of both sides based on theories. Criticism requires professional knowledge and must be fair.

There are times when reviews for your creations bring you a favorable message. That is, because of the criticism, more people are interested in listening to your creation, as well as building a broader discourse about it. Therefore, based on these two reasons, you will get free publicity for your creation. If so it's an unexpected advantage.

Thus, after a period of six months or a year, you can start a way to advertise your creations on the Internet (YouTube channel). It can also be acquired at no cost to you, and you must agree to certain rules for that permission. You can launch a campaign for your new video through other channels and pages in Facebook that include different music. That way, you can get some publicity for your new creation or video through this message to a wider group of friends than the group of friends on your Facebook account. As a result of your campaign, the number of subscribers will increase initially on your YouTube channel. The reason for this is that ninety percent of your campaign is still for a group of your friends whom you know. After some time, you will encounter a group of people you don't know. It is their reactions that you should refer to that will confirm the depth and quality of your playing. At this time, there will be a moment when you will receive very unfair reviews, especially on the Internet. Because people can post informal and very harsh and insulting comments without mentioning their proper names, those who hide them must be determined to put up with the obstacles and realize that there is no substance to them. As Dale Carnegie says, "nobody beats a dead dog". You must also have strong self-confidence and strong self-strength to move forward from those invalid reviews. Remember that you are being criticized because there is even a fair or shadow of progress in you in those creations. Naturally, such informal or unfair comments are presented every moment because of the fear that you will be a challenge to someone who is always ahead of his ability or knowledge. The reason for this is that people who do not have the strength and knowledge to overcome the challenges that come their way are rallying for unreasonable interruptions without any plan. Understand never ever be such a violent critic. Best answer for such brutal criticism for your creation is silence. Be careful not to strain yourself for any step other than being a performer and representing that role in the journey.

For videos released on the Internet (YouTube), never advertise for a contribution (subscribe) from the audience, because when you have presented your new opinion as a new wave that the audience has not heard, you should first check if there is a group of people who support or like your opinion of the new wave. Giving something that the listener likes or expects will not create a new wave and the listener may admire such things, but it is not done regarding your opinion on the new wave. So, as a test of your opinion or the new wave, you quietly release your creation on the Internet and wait. If someone listens to your creation of a new trend and subscribes, it will be very successful and it will help you in your future journey. You cannot force the listener to enjoy or be entertained by your creation. Attempting to do so will only fail you as a player.

For such creations, even if the first results are very little, being satisfied with them will be effective for your stability as well as for a further step. In the same way, it is very easy to subscribe first for this new wave of yours and it should be spread meaningfully through your Facebook on electronic media. If you do not have a proper understanding of it, you should do a study on it or seek the help of an experienced person or organization who has a good knowledge of marketing or advertising media and who has a lot of experience in handling it well. If the videos you have released on your channel (YouTube) contain a conservative or traditional playing genre, the channel you started as a beginner does not have a strong presence for such videos. Even after many years, very few views are added to it and there is no review about it. Because there are too many such videos on the internet [YouTube] and the listener shows very little interest in such music. There is a demand for the instruments of players who use conservative traditions that are well-known or in a strong position in the world because of the reputation that they have built up over many years. Sometimes you will see that they have made some minor changes in such performances. Therefore, remember that you must include a change or a new trend in your playing for a step forward. No matter how long these pieces traditional and common have been on the Internet, there is no growth in the listeners' attention to those pieces, and the listeners' contribution and criticism are not added for that.

All this may seem like a challenge to you. Remember that there is no depth or meaning in a process without challenge. If you are not prepared for such a journey, you will reach the end of your journey without any strength or a solid foundation as a player. It should be the result and goal of a musician to reach such a range in the music field, which is not limited to a small environment and covers the entire world.

This way, after six months or a year of posting your creations online, you can start a Fan Page by linking to your Facebook. Remember that Fan Page is more professional than Facebook. Through it, you can launch a wider campaign about your creations. If possible, try to record an interview with some renowned players in the field on your mobile phone and post it on the page. Try to discuss the content of your new wave creations as much as possible. The message you used to launch, the various techniques used for it, the major difference in your composition, and the tones rhythms, extended techniques used for it, should be widely discussed in the discussion and try to make the listener understand it.

When any opportunity arises be ready to present your performance of some of your new wave creations for successful concerts, even if it is for a very small group. This is a great opportunity to socialize with them. Appreciate the great opportunity first, aside from showing interest in charging money for your performances in such concerts. Conquering the concert stage is one of the strongest qualities of a performer, and in such cases, it will be an experience for you. Even if the concert was a small crowd, it will also allow you to capture your small group of fans and chat with them after the show. It's a great opportunity for a player, and your popularity is at least as important to your survival as fans are interested in connecting with an artist. Keep in mind that many strong things are made of small things. Therefore, this transaction over time is the function that advances a performer's journey.

In the meantime, if you can participate in a radio program, an article in a newspaper or a music magazine, and a television program, it is a great help for your next step. Keep in mind that it's not that hard to get this kind of publicity for a new wave that you've built and are eager to launch. Never give up on trying socializing with the new wave. Even if many of the things you are looking for, such as socializing this wave, are not available, there will be an opportunity to spread it differently and unexpectedly, because much is given to the seeker. So never give up the search or pursuit. As mentioned earlier, a play with a difference has more appetite and demand than a regular play and has more space in newspapers, magazines, radio, and television channels. Because they are looking for fresh things and prefer to present fresh things to society then their media will get wide publicity. Such a new wave is for them to have the label of being socialized. This clearly shows that at every moment, somewhere in the world, new products, new concepts, and new genres are emerging, and the media and the entire human race are alert to them. Any musician who makes the effort to advance using the techniques in this book would do well. There are many books like this available in the world. You can change people. Concepts can be changed. It will carry a wonderful message to society. Shouldn't it be? How precious is the struggle of a lifetime for that change? See the world's strongest individuals. Study them. They have reached that position by offering some service, investment, or message to humanity itself. However, you cannot get there without doing any work.

One will be limited to five thousand friends on Facebook. If you start another Facebook like this, you can have five thousand more friends, but don't do it and go to a LinkedIn profile. A LinkedIn profile is a professional landing page for you to manage your own, personal brand. The mission of LinkedIn is simple, connect the world's professionals and make them more productive and successful. Although LinkedIn is usually suitable for a professional musician, you can start very small and connect with several different people in your field who are interested in players and composers as your friends. Be careful to start everything small. You are sure to gain strength over time. Likewise, gradually enter social networks like Instagram, TikTok, X, Mastodon and then launch a supporting foundation. You can gain more popularity with TikTok. Don't be afraid of the concept of thinking big. You should think like that. Then it will be implemented, and a result will be experienced. You are always open worldwide no matter how small you are.

The group of 5,000 friends you acquire on Facebook is the result of a promotional medium used to launch your new wave. Making room for five thousand more friends there or starting another new Facebook page won't get you the exposure or publicity you're looking for. What happens is that an unnecessary group of people who do not represent your field join you. Make sure that there is no omission or delay on your part. The practice or experience gained in this way will be greatly integrated into the procedure of progress in the future.

LinkedIn was founded on May 5, 2003, by Reid Hoffman and Allen Blue two American businessmen [it is now owned by Microsoft] and it is considered the world's largest professional network with 930 million members in 200 countries. The network is limited to thirty thousand of the world's most powerful professionals as friends in any field. Anyone can enter and join the network, but the ability to make friends and apply for friendship depends on the strength you have built as a player, conductor, teacher or composer. This will enable anyone to build an international network. If the new wave you have created as a player is strong, if his path is meaningful, there should be no fear or doubt about socializing through it. Because it has been mentioned earlier in this book that it is easy to socialize such a change or a new wave of playing at a time when the listener is often concerned about something new or meaningful.

It is very important to have a small group of people when starting or planning to socialize with the new wave. For this purpose, five thousand is a large group and it is somewhat difficult to acquire or gather such a group because all of them should be knowledgeable and interested in music. Therefore, settle for that meaningful group. Try different ways advertising rather than just limiting to one. Identify those ways. Develop a quest or plan first to act. Don't follow everyone else's footsteps and try to find new ways. Any person who has built a new trend has an innate knowledge of such new techniques. Try to live in a dimension where there is no limit to defeat. Then defeat will be chased away from the back door and victory will embrace you.

These are the times when society, man, and nature often cross or collide to create a new wave that moves forward. You who are creating a new trend in any field, must have a strong understanding and align to avoid those events and overcome those events, if not the journey will be weakened. Don't let even an iota of such a concept enter your mind or procedure. Follow the famous Japanese saying, "If you fall seven times, get up eight times". You can't succeed in a stable journey without falling. It is a common occurrence in this kind of journey. Anyone who is rallying in front of the determination to overcome extraordinary events must be acutely aware of such minor delays or temporary defeats. Where is victory in the world without defeat? In such defeats, there is hidden a most powerful message that no intellectual or powerful book can convey that you have not thought of or seen before. It is easy for anyone who has embarked on a vigorous journey to discover it. Shouldn't the alignment be the framework of a new wave, making the difficult things easy, defeating and winning unexpected goals? Anyone who steps into that frame will be blessed to touch and embrace the unseen and unimagined. One would be afraid to step into that frame. The most powerful medicine in the world to overcome fear is to act on the cause of the fear. If so, isn't what is in front of you the world that has been around for a long time that you expected to enter? Are you ready?

The important thing that every person who makes a change in any field should understand is that he cannot change the entire human race according to his taste or opinion. His opinion or wave cannot be obeyed by everyone. You live in a society or a world full of different cultures, tastes, and attitudes. Therefore, if you have decided to cover all these human generations with your new wave, it will fail. One part of it can be a large crowd. They will bow their head to your idea. That's your achievement. Don't worry about moving on. Because history has proven that no one in the world can please everyone. Avoid making the mistake of changing these concepts. The same goes for you. Therefore, you should be in a group that sells your new wave, and you should be satisfied with that group.

There are no two people in this world who have the same ideas. It is a topic not suitable for debate and its true man must be understood. Living in the world is one task. Living with a good understanding of life is another task. If the latter were mandatory, the world would surely become a meaningful place. Therefore, the latter is mandatory for you as a player. Because as you said before, you are a player with a different wave who strives to undergo some transformations in the human concepts that are lined up to convey a meaningful message through your creations into the human mind. The player must have a deep understanding of this and be aligned to strive for such an endeavor.

No one person is ever the same on the outside as well as on the inside. You are a person with instincts like no other in the world. Therefore, everyone else in the world is also the same. Such people cannot be converted to other concepts or new thinking by any other means than intelligence. When a man and a woman meet as lovers, they exaggerate and pretend to highlight their talents and assert, although the day when they start to live together under one roof reality will be realized to each other and there could be some misunderstandings in their relationship. If the wisdom and its understanding are so powerful among them this type of incident never occurs.

Any player can change the listener through his mastered instrument. For this purpose, he manages the instrument he owns, controls it, unveils new concepts, and makes use of the meaningful tones emanating from the creation, along with the strong bond he has built up with the instrument. For this reason, it is extremely important to look at the performer's career in the time devoted to the instrument. Therefore, the time you spend with your instrument is the main factor for your success.

Today, various people, groups, companies, and institutions are running several services on the Internet to popularize music, develop social media connections, and lend a helping hand to players. Most of these are free and are useful not only for the new wave player but for any musician of any skill level. Some services collect money, and it is not important for you to be interested in them in the beginning. Keep in mind that most of these organizations are not providing proper service unless they are paid. Visit social media services and release a creation or two of your new waves. This will give you a great opportunity to listen to your music as well as see your performance in foreign countries, especially in your home country. Once you've reached the stage where your performance can be streamed, you can also connect with the world's live performances online. Since live concerts cannot be held in times of epidemics, these newly launched online connections are increasing nowadays, and using them is a great opportunity for you. For this, technological tools are expensive and as a performer, it is very important to gather such gear during your journey and prepare for taking part in such events. Some of these live performances are paid for but without based on money, try to give a prominent place to promote your new wave from the start.

Often man waits for the future to plan his future. They commonly get ready to plan the future by saying tomorrow or next week or next month or next year or from the 1st of January. Remember that your future is determined by what you bring to your existence today. Therefore, remove the concept of tomorrow and direct your strongest action to today or the present. In this way, you will get the valuable future that you are looking for. So don't miss every small opportunity to socialize with the new trend of a player. Often people are not satisfied with a simple process and are aligned with the idea of always turning to the deeper things. Sometimes it’s tragic if you don’t get such fruitful opportunities. It is right to be tempted to achieve a large range through thinking broadly about one's existence. But when many positive events come together, it will be a strong investment. It is mandatory for you who have planned a long journey to be satisfied with even such a small achievement or small development. Often this kind of positive development that will make your journey successful is around you, but it will not be recognized by many who do not have a strong goal. Therefore, you must have such a vision. It can only be recognized by a character with such a mindset. If you too have embarked on a powerful journey, you must be prepared to look at events with an open mind and watchful eyes in such small opportunities. So never let the targeted journey in your thoughts slip away. It is caused by your thoughts or mind. You should be aware of this. Power cannot be attained without the use of knowledge.

In socializing the new wave of playing, setbacks, obstacles, and difficulties are not absent. You should consider it something meaningful or something natural that arises when socializing change. Such dark moments depend only for a short time. Then again, the present will become bright for the future. As a beginner, you should recognize such opportunities and setbacks and not get confused by them. No event or existence is uniform. If it happens, no one will see any transformation or change in the world. Nature, environment, man, products, and thought are all in change and human existence and action collide with the changes. It blends in with this change unconsciously and as a result, will embrace the new wave of your playing. In a changing world, if the music remains unchanged, it will not be surprising that it will gradually disappear from the hands of the listeners. Because man faces changes and expects those changes and that change becomes a habit. Human embraces these things that society labels as behavior, whether they are good or bad.

Reflect on the resources you have and stop thinking about the resources you don't have. It is bound to be an obstacle to one's progress in the long run. Then thinking about what you don't have often will overtake your actions. Then one's journey, determination, goal, or purpose will slowly become blurred as a result of one's thinking not towards a strong step but a minimal assessment. Sometimes it will be broken beyond repair. So always keep your eyes, mind, and ears open, and don't let yourself lose sight of the goal. Therefore, in many fields of the world, the strong are seen to be lonely, busy, and away from others. The number of friends such greats have is very minimal because they don't have time to spend with friends. Likewise, it is a difficult matter. They have very little interest in picnics, conferences, festivals, and sports competitions. They surf the Internet and social media networks on Facebook, not just for fun, but to fulfill their goals or objectives. Most people who see this may understand that he is wasting time for fun. Because most people surf a media network for their entertainment. But social media is a great investment for anyone. However, he uses the social media network as a market and takes proper advantage of it, and is maintained proper management. He becomes a commodity there and engages in the work of selling himself. He enters the thoughts or opinions of its members and grasps them to his opinion. Make proper use of social media networks. Whether there is a new wave in the music or not, you as a player should initiate such a move. You should tell them who you are. But remember, you can get into their hearts only if you as a player have some strength in your playing. Otherwise, it's no wonder they reject you. Release your message first. Then you come forward. Without it, it is a futile attempt to make the mistake of getting ahead of you in the first place.

Creating a change in playing that will keep the listener attached is no easy task. It is a work that comes out after a long study by undergoing some sacrifices. In addition to the analysis of the practice of cultivating it in this book, you should also make some additions to highlight your work. It's a great opportunity to showcase your uniqueness in a way that no one else has. Then its content or shape and space will see a perfect finish. That's what should happen. In this way, the happiness that you get at the end of launching such a task and the results that emerge from it are immense. It will be very effective for your future. It is a blessing to be a player at such a level.

When socializing a new wave of your playing, it must use a well-managed and deeply planned methodology. It is important to connect with an experienced person or group in the field of advertising media if your knowledge is limited. An organization with such a person or group may charge an unaffordable amount for that work. Since a player starting his playing career cannot afford such money, the player must acquire knowledge of sales or business management. There are huge number of books available in the market that containing facts about this, but one will be able to acquire the facilities free of charge after taking membership in a library. However, for a musician who has started his playing career and is trying to popularize a new wave, he needs to have knowledge and awareness about marketing and management. You have to think about modern methods to market your new trend. Therefore, it is effective to focus on this task before or at the time of socializing a new wave of playing.

Your acquaintances with people from all walks of life are important for this work. Be anxious to gather such a group. Students studying from you and their parents will lend you a helping hand for this task. When your friends, relatives, and parents gather, you will form a small strong group for any initiative, and remember that you cannot plan a long trip with that group. Therefore, start planning everything small and slowly. No matter how long the journey is, it must begin with taking the first step. No one can ever think of such a long journey as that first step. One should be happy with this small beginning and think of it as a proper beginning.

Bittersweet and awkward times don't last forever for anyone. Life must go through certain periods. These periods are not eternal and such moments can be considered periods for the well-planning of your existence. The benefit from such an opportunity is immense. Likewise, one can look back and be happy at the end. Victory after defeat is always eternal. Such people often become qualified to give advice and counsel to others.

Serious setbacks, defeats, and failures are inevitable before a strong victory. No one will excel who has not overcome such things. One would think that this happens only in the field of playing that you represent. For you who always think like that, even a small setback may be stronger than another huge collapse of society. It's not because of the subject you represent. You lack understanding of problems.

You can never launch something on faith alone. As the launch of a new wave of playing, you must have some practical method to turn it into a stable success. In addition to the methods that everyone else uses, you may use new or other methods that you build on your trust. Sometimes they have made progress with the methods others have used, but it may not be possible or compatible with you. There is no need to have any doubt or fear about this. Because the seeker finds what he seeks. When you keep an eye on this, it's natural for ideas and new trends to flow to you. Thoughts arise only if there are preparations or such views. Through the control of your mind, you can control it well for a wish that you have sought, and this long-term event will show the mind the best opportunities to enter new paths that will open your way. You can't see ahead before implementing something. But you, who have been playing the role of a player for a long time, have faced such incidents many times. See how they line up perfectly. You should not have any doubt or fear about it. With such a controlled mindset, you'll find successful strategies align well over time. When you have such a meaningful and powerful journey, society will also join you. Most people are ready to have relationships with such characters.

When socializing a change in playing, never look at your past and make decisions. That past is probably a painful past full of failed attempts. Bury that past forever. Think successfully about the present. The practices you put your mind into action today and the methods used to make that action a reality will elevate you to a level you never imagined. This process will give your future a solid foundation. Think and think hard. Never let that thought slip away from you. Always strive to be one or two steps ahead of others. The results you get in the long run are tremendous.

Anyone strong in any field in the world will confirm that they have moved forward with the support of others. Therefore, you must have such a group. This is something that cannot be done in one day at once. For that, you must be prepared for a long time. You must have a powerful process that you build in addition to the discourse of creating your new wave and publishing it or socializing it. You must search. Experimentation, research, and some excerpts are suitable for this purpose, and many meaningful things will often touch you in the process of launching this experiment. They may be processes that are unique to you and have not been used before. The benefits of discoveries using new methods are more appropriate than the old conservative ones and will suit the rapidly changing society. A changing society needs new and different thoughts. Its effectiveness will also increase and society looking for new concepts will embrace it. Even if these new methods have shortcomings, they will be seen through your experience, and you will be able to correct them. Because the experiences you have gained during the time you are trying to socialize with this new wave are very powerful.

What you know is of no use to you, until you apply it in a useful way for your existence, don't hide your knowledge without using it and store it like money. You must use that knowledge and market yourself. Today the entire universe is a market. Therefore, you must represent that market. Happy if you have something for sale there. If it is something strongly different, it is very satisfying and productive. The purpose of the performer is to make those powerful things for the enjoyment or satisfaction of another group. In this way, you can market your knowledge well and establish your existence in that market.

After a long journey as a player, you have popularized a new wave of playing, and you are a player who can claim a unique playing style that you have built. When you come to this level, you own about 90% of the creation and control of what you have planned. If not, or if you imitate others, it will never be a new wave of performance. It will be a common wave or a common playing style that has been heard before in the field of play. Therefore, controlling yourself after that awakening is the main factor that happens to you. Never let it get damaged. Currently, reject almost all the methods of critics and various people who are friendly to you. With such an identity, the opinions, thoughts, and suggestions of others are not able to continue this process. Because you are the one who gave birth to that new wave.

It includes your identity or your name that complements your abilities. As soon as another idea or thought enters it, its rhythm, shape, style, growth, and novelty will be broken. Your fan or listener will understand it instantly. Because what remains in your fan's memory is the essence of your playing or the style you have built with great effort. If it breaks, the relationship between you and your fan will break. Keep in mind that you live in a society full of people who strive to be intelligent in front of people who excel in any field of society. Don't be gullible to those views.

Much of what you use to create the level or background you live in today is your thoughts. Don't leave it to someone to spoil or change it today. For you, who are well acquainted with its present rule, do not agree with their ideas. Avoid giving advice and advice to anyone who has strength in any field, especially in a subject other than the field of music. Because you have a deep knowledge of your field of play, its contents or the methods used for your powerful journey are not suitable for other fields at all.

Usually, it is natural for someone to start with you or to get close to you and offer various ideas and suggestions for your betterment. But long-suffering, researching, bumping, and having plenty of experience, you'll realize as soon as it's uttered that the admonitions don't fit. So don't worry about such an experiment. There are so many invaluable self-help and motivate books available in the market today and you can gain what you expect by reading those books. Having embarked on a successful journey, it will often be a challenge for you to try such changes today. Likewise, your new wave is likely to suffer from it as well. Make sure that the background or deep meaning layer that has been built up over a long period of effort is never broken. Don't fall back in the background of striving to move forward while protecting that plane. Reflect often on the experiences and methods you have encountered so far in the field and the new course. Strive to make them firmer on the path you are on. There is no practice or achievement without effort.

Even if you have some existence in the field in your youth through performing, it is temporary and it disappears from society as you grow older, and building it up in this period of your life is some serious work. If you get into a new wave at a young age, eventually it will reach a certain depth and you will be able to experience many things. Even if a famous player maintains some presence or popularity in society, that popularity is often not so permanent. They are players who have been awarded by a group of loyal or friendly people on the very popular social media. Many people can easily build their popularity on Facebook. Some are satisfied with the favorable comments you receive on Facebook and do not reflect your identity or the truth of what you are capable of. It simply contains a shallow environment of lamentation, happiness, news, humor, and love among friends, and does not express the correctness of your playing or your existence. Anyway, some players maintain a powerful existence on Facebook with well balance methods during their playing career. This is not the fault of that social media platform. This is the fault of your system or the way you handle it. Your propaganda must be very modern, accurate, and broad to fit into YouTube as it has more serious viewers and critics than other such social media. Likewise, you can access a wide audience through a LinkedIn profile, which is a network of professionals. It is a network built for the most powerful professionals in the world in any field. The depth of your creations is well critiqued there. Also, TikTok is a very popular platform gives your new trend more propaganda.

Never try to judge the current state or level of your playing because you are performing for a group of fans or listeners. Therefore, the status of that play should be decided by them. As mentioned before, avoid rating someone based on the responses on Facebook or through the opinions of his friends, relatives, and his students. One may be a famous teacher who often teaches music. A music teacher may be involved in a school, institute, or university system. Teaching is one job. Playing is another task. No matter how popular a teacher is, his playing skills may not be matched with teaching. It is another field as deep as teaching.

Precious teachings are rare in the world. Such precious playing is also rare in the world. Teaching is the imparting of subject knowledge, concepts, and practices to an eager group of learners. It also means providing any advice, knowledge, or subject and helping the student who wants to learn. Method of teaching, wisdom and the knowledge of that subject must combine together for fine teaching. A player or performing means direct enjoyment of a listener or a group of listeners. These two subjects represent two contradictory levels. Therefore, a player should determine the current state of his playing or the level by available criticisms based on correct analysis and wisdom.

The facts are thus only from the in-depth or intelligent reviews you get on the internet for your playing or from the opinion of reviewers who have acquired knowledge about that play that you should get an idea to standardize your music. One cannot judge one's playing by using hugely popular comments or with several views. Popularity is one. The depth of that music is on another level. Both are two contradictory situations.

If you want, you can get a huge number of views and a huge number of subscribers for your channel on the internet [YouTube] in no time. This can be done by giving what the listener is asking for most. But there will be no identity of you at all. It only happens that you, like them, enter a common ground where many people live in the world. This kind of thing will not be suitable for your existence if you do not strive to fulfill the duties that should be expected of you after entering the field of performing. Following another style or another group of people will not reflect even a semblance of your own identity.

The increase in the number of fans for the sake of the player's existence or popularity will be a powerful support to your playing career. Therefore, you must be smart when dealing with your fans. Be very careful, if your words or actions involve things that hurt them, they will leave you. In a world of mass followers, you should be satisfied with having a small group of fans and you should be eager to improve that number. No matter how strong your playing is or what kind of intensity it contains, if your routine or relationship with the fans falls apart, they will leave you. Therefore, when you enter something on your Facebook or the Internet (YouTube, Spotify, Apple music, Amazon music), or any other social media network or streaming services you should think wisely about the way that you communicate with them. Then the strength of your playing will stand out and you also will be properly socialized.

Many players in the field of music that you represent are involved in the activities of their playing career. Likewise, many new players are joining the field every day and you should have a proper understanding of this before introducing a new wave of your playing. When a fan is satisfied with your playing and joins you, he will be associated with you and your playing for the rest of his life. You should have a well-thought plan to retain such fans with you. The plan refers to the good and proper management of your field.

YOUR EXISTENCE

Chapter 6

"The end of the preparation should be the performance".

It is natural for you to feel disheartened when something is missed or delayed. But when you realize that you can't get back what you missed, you will feel a lot of anxiety and pain. You have come to this world to do mighty work. Coming here will be pointless if any area is left untouched or unfulfilled. It doesn't matter what status you were born on. Many people say that status is sad, resource-poor, lonely, or full of difficulty and there is no chance for a step forward and they live a pathetic life in it and leave their lives. More than 80% percent of the world billionaires started their career in this pathetic atmosphere. The resources available to every human being in the world are immense. It is invisible to someone indifferent or disinterested in it. Many things must be done upside down for their survival. You must be selective about your goals. Goals should be established. Those goals and objectives should be put to proper use without delay. Childhood, youth, middle age, and twilight are all to be met in due course. What should be done in childhood or school age should be completed at that age and cannot be done in the twilight of one's life. Life is like a mountain that is built step by step. After the first step is the second step. You should be ready for that. When stepping on a staircase, if you do not step in order, you cannot take a step over five or six steps at a time. It cannot be done that way. Such an attempt is both unsuccessful and fearful. You plan your playing career step by step like this. Then all this will build up step by step. Step fitness will keep you strong as a giant for life. Then you will be socialized as a strong character or a character that has confirmed your proper existence.

The powerful player of the world, who recognized the role of the musician, passed away in this manner. Their music will forever be etched in human hearts for years to come. There will be a discussion about it.

In the production of goods, the manufacturer must fulfill the needs of the customer. There, the manufacturer is very interested in his customer, not only the quality of the product but also its shape, color, longevity, and age-appropriate nature, after a strong study of many things, he manufactures a much better-quality product than what is available in the market today. With these qualities, the sales of that product will surpass other products. In the same way, the player or the composer should take a step forward. He must socialize something that he can conclude as an idea, a feeling that the listener has never heard before, a sound, a rhythm, a style, or a color perfected in a new style. Using a style that has been in play for years is very similar to the attempt by another company to re-produce the same product and enter the market. But with a new wave, he will transform the listener's ideas and concepts like never before, and thus popularize the meaningful and profound message of the player or composer. In the production of a product, by producing it that is already in the market and the manufacturer does not have a competitive advantage or a huge benefit or publicity. Although there are many similar sweet drinks such as Coca-Cola in the world market, none of them could surpass the production of Coca-Cola due to their modern and attractive propaganda. The musician remains popular with his new trend of playing in the field of giving what the listener likes or appreciates. There must be a difference in his creation like the new product. However, if the new wave is not visible in his composition, he is the result of an effort made by many people in different fields of the world to stay on a common level. Failing to adopt any of the new concepts as explained in this book, your career as a performer will ultimately end as an attempt to label you as a follower rather than a new trend or style of your playing, as previously mentioned. First, you need to understand the difference or contrast between the work of producing a product and composing or creating a piece of music. But there is what you can gain by studying corporate giants in the world and their sales methods, new visions of the products, propaganda, and the practices of capturing the market.

A commodity provides the necessary facilities to sustain a man's daily life and by listening to a powerful piece of music, the brain activity of a man directly increases his mental development including his action system and thinking. Therefore, by listening to a piece of music, the functions of developing your memories, solving a powerful brain comparison process, as an antidote for everyday diseases, strengthening the thinking process, activating every part of the brain, and awakening lost memories are the main factors.

None of these mental statuses can't be acquired, by buying a consumer product from the market. Therefore, isn't the performer offering to society or the entire human race a powerful set of virtues? As a performer, your new wave is more than just entering the market with a new product, society often offers many unknown processes to the entire human race. How important mental development is for human survival, will be confirmed when we look at the books written by famous philosophers throughout history. Research on thought and its existence are huge in books and research that are published frequently in the world. Therefore, in addition to that, this message given by the musician to the entire human race cannot be compared with any other product or merchandise.

Creating and releasing valuable powerful things to society is a difficult task. But a strong player socializes the tasks well by summarizing his long stay in the field, his experience in playing and his popularity, and his connections.

Check out the giants of the Baroque Period (1600-1750) such as J.S. Bach, Antonio Vivaldi, Friedrich Handel, and the giants of the Classical Period (1750-1820) such as Beethoven, Mozart, and Hayden. Today's composers of that style have failed to surpass such compositions, no matter how rich and complex the world's inventions are. Anyway, there is a famous saying that 'good musician is a dead musician'. You must study all these in your attempt to socialize something and never let that attempt fail. There are so many opportunities and chances for such experimental research. The resources are also available in abundance for such studies. Then you are less likely to make excuses for failure. Where thought, determination, competitiveness, and sheer will come together, failure will crumble.

Your path to success lies in your ability to recognize the message in failures, breakdowns, and defeats. That space builds powerfully within you based on your willpower and heroism, which were previously discussed in this book. To one who has such goals, the tremendous messages in these failures or defeats become visible. Opportunities and resources do not line up at your feet. But this is a moment where such an opportunity has lined up. Man, often worships in anticipation of a future event. Lessons learned from defeat or failures are not worshiped. These experiences are an advantage that you do not have to worship. There are always two sides to a coin. Both sides are equal in value. Because when the two sides of the coin are added, its value is added.

The resources that build up in the peaceful and intelligent atmosphere are limitless. A person who is neither peaceful nor intelligent cannot build up such high-powered resources. These resources are extremely important for your creativity, especially for building a new wave.

You must be careful when dealing with people. As stated earlier, don't worry about getting to know people, which is the hardest thing in the world. It is a very complex task but not easy. It's especially important to network with players in your field but be very careful about associating with them. Being friends with them for a long time is important for your survival. But you must reject various oppressive actions, defiant behavior patterns, and unfair criticisms of people with different opinions and characteristics in society. Likewise, the various changes bestowed upon us by nature are often harmful. Thirdly, some of your decisions, thoughts, and behaviors are aligned for this confused existence and it is beneficial for you to have some understanding of these threefold processes. By being in this profession for a period you will surely understand this very well as you encounter these occasions and events from time to time. From time to time, you will meet people in your field who have defiant behavior patterns, which is the first of the above tasks. You should be aware of them. Such people near you are more dangerous than the enemy far away. Be careful not to collide with them. That is not your work or existence. Beyond that, you should step up for a very robust procedural journey. Similarly, anyone who advances in any field of the world faces many objections and obstacles from society and man. No one has entered a path of victory without much opposition and obstacles. It would be strange if it went on without interruption. In this journey, you should deal with your decisions, thoughts, and behaviors mentioned thirdly. Be careful with your comments. Remember that once something has been said, it will seriously damage your life to apologize or withdraw it if the statement is inappropriate. Minimize your expressions during a discussion. Others will fear your silence and be confused by the powerful message embedded in your secrecy. Give short answers at the right time and place. Because you are a player with a new wave, not a critic. Imagine that you can only express yourself through your mastered musical instrument. Show it to the community. Unveil anything that is an attack on society, an attack on humanity through your mastered musical instrument.

Double-check your decision-making. Here is your chance to implement it or try it out. So don't worry. In a calm mind, foresight will not waver and will be very calm and comfort you.

Therefore think. Never try to delegate your decisions to others. Don't let others control you. Your thoughts are yours. It is a new and different wave of thought. Let it socialize. Your opinion is not socialized if any other controls you or convinces you. Listening to their inner patterns of some meaningful and different thoughts may be comforting to you but avoid embracing them too strongly.

It is quite difficult to get advice from one of the world's strongest or top-level players. It is quite a difficult task as they are busy, and many people live in foreign countries. But if you try it will not be a difficult task. The advice of such people is very accurate, and the content is relevant to today's playing field. For this purpose, watch some videos on the internet (YouTube) of such players who represent your instrument or have mastered the instrument. You'll often get free Zoom meetings with workshops and advice from the world's top performers. Watch out for that.

Here are the second negative effects that nature gives you and you should also be concerned about alleviating them. It also needs to be remedied and such changes affect society thoroughly, do not be shocked by it. For example, a very hot day will hamper your training. That extreme heat will directly affect your instrument, which is your most valuable asset. Protecting your instrument is also very important. And on a day when there is heavy rain, the sound of the rain will mix with the sound of your instrument, and you will not get a proper standard and meaningful sound. Having a home studio in your home won't hurt you at all. In the same way, the surrounding environment will not hear the sound through a studio, so there will be no disturbance to the neighbors. Although the tools for that are expensive, slowly get it done over time. Such resources should be acquired during the journey launched in the playing career, because it's very useful for your progress.

Any person representing any field should leave a meaningful and powerful message to society at the end of his life journey. It is the responsibility of mankind. Everyone in society has the capacity for it and no one can shirk their duty. But when you look at society, you will surely understand that it is not going well. It is tragic.

As a player, you may have picked up your musical instrument as a child, or maybe at the young age. After staying with the instrument for such a long time, gaining a great experience, gaining a reputation for playing, building a group of listeners with different cultural patterns, and owning the label of a player, what is the essence of it if a new wave of change is not included in the playing? A performance that does not contain such a difference will be lost very quickly in the hands of the people. How many such musicians are there in the province or country where you live? Do a little research on them. As they pass away, their music will be buried with them. Everyone in the world must say goodbye when the time comes. It cannot be avoided. But even after a new wave player leaves the society, his playing will not be the same. Their playing will be immortal.

In society, we meet people who are stubborn, tough, and unyielding and have negative effects on themselves and society. Never attempt to correct them. It is not suitable for a player in a world of fast-paced technology, growth, and innovation. It is inappropriate to pursue such people while the musician is on a sharp and decisive journey with his unique outlook. There is no time for that. The performer will also meet people in society who are half asleep and do not have the strength to understand the deep things. They deserve to be your listener. Therefore, they should be shifted from where they are to a higher place. One more member will join hands with other members (fans) as he can understand your opinion or difference. In the meantime, the player will also meet people who are looking for understanding or knowledge. Educate them. Ninety percent of the time they will join hands with you. Join this group. They will be directly connected to uplifting your new wave. No one in this world has progressed in any field without the support of others. The same goes for you who represent the role of a player. Be a silent character in your presence and appearance (without acting) but fast in action, strong-willed, pursuing new goals, and working most of the day as an active machine. All that has become great in the world are those who have perfected such things.

Never, ever, avoid matching or emulating yourself with any other character or person. It directly destroys one's own identity and destroys the incomparable abilities and uniqueness that are innately built into you. Often people try to play the characters of a favorite movie or novel in their real life. How tragic to follow a fictional character created by its creator. Often such characters are not seen or heard in the society you live in, and one should investigate the factors that caused such characters to have such a deep impact on one's existence. Otherwise, not only will one's identity be broken, but the character that is built by birth or strives to be built by such a person will be a complete failure. One's own or inherent journey, shape, thought pattern, ability to absorb or understand something, fresh thinking about the future, and self-strength consists of many things and avoid spoiling the precious things that are made of that nature. All this is very detrimental to a player who is looking for a new wave of playing. It is a procedure that is not suitable for someone who is looking for a change in any field. You must build your own identity and you may get very little support from others. When you reach the high level of any subject you are always alone, because very seldom you find a person can give you advice or an idea about your powerful activities. Specially regarding your creation with a new style. Keep in mind that the musician's creativity is built on his thought and practice and a thorough understanding of his instrument. A well-studied musical instrument can breathe new life or a new wave through its use based on thought and practice. Then one is not alone or isolated and, on this energy, there is no hindrance to reaching the desired plane.

If the growth of your new wave of content stalls as your audience joins you in experiencing the new trend of your music, it will directly affect your survival. Because they can only go with you as far as you can go. The listeners cannot go beyond you. Because they don't have a deep understanding or philosophy of playing as you do. Therefore, frequent freshness should be included in your compositions. As a result, your fans will rally around you and new fans will join this group. No one likes to experience monotony for long. Aging, growing intelligence, changing social attitudes, and your creation should also lead to some changes in shape and nature.

A player should never be satisfied with his performance. Because then he will not strive to represent a higher level than the current level or for a future vision. It should happen that way. Most of the philosophies involve being satisfied with one's given abilities. But such ideas have transformed into outdated ideas of playing today. If you don't accept these challenges, your existence will fail because of a failure of growth. Few overcome such challenges. But indeed, they are winners. You too can achieve these achievements. Therefore, the word "little" should be removed from your usage and it should be highlighted that it is attainable for all. Most of the individuals who achieved success use the same methodology. Only the essence (flavor) should change. The player is ready to please someone. If you understand the essence of that view, you have understood the proper truth of the play. Then your foundation will also be successful.

Most of the time, people live by following the common behavior of society, the methods that are used today. There is some setback in trying to get out of it and take a new path, and it is stuck in that range without trying to go beyond it. Many people are limited to a small environment and imprisoned in that space and waste time and energy. They are afraid to get out of that small range and go to other concepts or thoughts. Apart from that, understanding another world and trying to enter that world is only limited to a few people. You who are going to a new path of playing must get out of it and enter that world. There are many methods available there. Without going far, you must first understand that you have all these resources around you or within you.

Understanding is a step toward change and will be an introduction to new concepts. It is the origin of powerful thought. Therefore, this understanding of a player is a valuable set of thoughts for him to enter a new path of playing and acquire a wide range. This thinking must be realistic with your natural inner thoughts. Using your smartphone too much can be a hindrance to your free thinking. Therefore, try to use your smartphone only for the necessary activities, such as your propaganda work or any other essential things without going beyond that.

Whether a woman or a man, he or she is the most valued, marketed, and prioritized person in the world. It is true that 'I' emerges before all others or everything. It is very common for a girlfriend or boyfriend to say to their loved one, 'I don't love anyone in this world as much as you'. There is no truth in it. No one in this world loves, appreciates, tries to protect, tries to sell to you as much as you do. Therefore, it is easy to raise your existence to a higher level based on your emergence or striving to socialize in that 'I' name. You should strive for that. It is a powerful thought that is instilled in you from birth. If so, you have a great opportunity to make it a lifelong theme and become a force. Merely manifesting the ego cannot make it powerful. It should be nurtured and brought out through some strong and meaningful process. No one can get close to or achieve the pinnacle of development at once. There is no information in history about anyone who has done so in any field. A long journey begins with one step. There are hundreds of thousands of steps to the top.

It is also not correct to conclude that it is the end. There is no end or end to progress. It is a continuous process. Therefore, progress is about acquiring what you want. It will never end. How long have you been waiting for an opportunity? No matter how long you wait, such an opportunity will never come. There are opportunities in front of the launched objective. They will lead you to the door of progress respectively. Therefore, you must launch something.

You may be half asleep. If so, you must wake up. Or maybe in deep sleep. If so when you wake up the delay is over you. You may be unaware. If so, you must be aware. Above all, you can be a stubborn character who does not care about others. Then you will not attain any prosperity. The choice is yours. No law in the world can change one's way of being. A hint or signal can be made about aligning properly for that meaningful and powerful presence. You can try this book for guidance. If so, you have the right to choose it. But the most important thing is that many of the great people of the world have achieved that position by using the knowledge of others and a procedure of their own.

Your defeats, breakdowns, and failures can be considered blessings during the beginning of your career. It is difficult for one who passes the twilight of life to come out of it again and make such vigorous efforts. Such energy should be established in the early stages. To cultivate this one must face various failures, breakdowns, and defeats. That kind of thing can get a temperament with a boost. If someone claims that he has not faced any such defeat, breakdown, or failure in his lifetime than it should be said that that person has not made any effort in his life for any socialization or such meaningful action. Remove relationships with such characters that have such thoughts from your company immediately. They will hinder your existence.

Many students do not engage in academic activities properly in school as well as in the university system. The main reason is the lack of proper planning and preparation for the future or future existence of such students. Because of these students, the university system will be undermined, and its depth will also collapse. Every person living in the world should have a good plan and proper understanding of their future journey. It should be established at school age. Must start at school. Students engage in various subjects in education and various activities in school, but there is no subject in the school recommendation sheet for the study of life or its management and existence. Concern about a most essential subject has been lost in the hands of educationists. A book published in 1925 by Bertrand Russell (1872 – 1970), a great philosopher of the twentieth century, the book called 'On Education' is an essential book that should be read by everyone who hopes to enter a university and in the field of education. Even though many years have passed, a good analysis has been done about its meaningful education.

Having done the task of socializing a new wave of music, you need to support it for a long time with the support of a group of people. If you have mastered an instrument and contributed to the task of teaching that instrument, this task will be easier for you. Because there is an opportunity to succeed in that process through your students, it will be successful based on the desire of the majority to play a style that is not popular in society or to use that style. People who see or hear that style will perceive it as a new wave created by you and that perception or discourse will make your name popular and long-lasting in that field.

Remember that the angry, hateful, critical words and comments that come out of your mouth burn or slow down your inner self. It should directly affect your creativity or the task of creating a new wave. Therefore, try to control the harmful thoughts that arise in your mind. The mind of a person who has embarked on a powerful journey and has a proper vision of it is free from such harmful ideas and concepts, because his thoughts are for free growth. Therefore, first, the value of being a player with such a mind should be understood and such a humble, decent, and well-sighted group should join in the field of music. Then many more people will join the field and the improvement of that field will surely reach a higher level. Everyone in the world is fighting for life. Like you, they are fighting the mighty battle of life. Exchanging such harmful words from them to you and from you to them is stopping the progress of both parties and engaging in other meaningless work. The performer can listen back and correct any flaws or weaknesses in the composition before launching it. But once a word is out of your mouth, it is impossible to correct it again. Similarly, after offering a composition to society, it cannot be changed again.

If you're right, no one remembers it. But if you are wrong, no one will forget it. That guilt will repeat itself and all your good deeds will be overshadowed. It is a habit of most of us to criticize other people's weaknesses and mistakes by neglecting them. It should be avoided as much as possible, because as mentioned earlier, criticism is inappropriate for you. Eventually, over time, it will become a habit of yours. It is very difficult to change habits that have been built up over a long period. Often you should be aware of your shortcomings, weaknesses, and setbacks and study them. In this way, we should think about the methods that can avoid those weaknesses. It is essential for the player's progress and survival. It is not a player's job to criticize or advocate for the shortcomings or weaknesses of others. First, acquire a comprehensive understanding of your range or your profession.

Life is a competition. You must participate in that. Tragically, only a fraction of the world's population participates in this competition. You must have a good understanding of the rules to be followed to win the competition. You can participate in it at any time on any day and you can also participate and leave the competition without anyone's permission. When you enter the competition, you can see a group of people who do not accept the rules of the competition and violate the terms by interfering with other competitors. There is no record in the history of such people going to the end of the competition. It is also very difficult to finish it in such a manner. Even if they win a small victory during the game, they are temporary. Even if the competition is thought to be difficult, no one has faced defeat by following proper and correct methods. You should also represent this way of competitive life. If you enter the competition with your new wave as the center, victory is easy. New technology and new techniques are often included in any game aiming at the winning path of that competition and the player needs to enter this field with his new wave. There are no shortcuts to success. But many great characters in the world shortened the path of victory by using successful and modern methods. Such methods cannot be acquired by society and those people finally acquire those systems through hard study and research. One can enter this path by looking at something with a sharp intellect, a keen eye, and understanding its essence well.

A person who has been a prominent representative of any field for a long time eventually will get to know the most successful methods and integrate those with the competition of life. The world is invented by combining two or more objects and the production process is successful, and the knowledge acquired by such successful people is used at various points in the journey to finish the race of life without defeat. If doubt and fear of experimentation and research are eliminated, such successful self-realization of resources does not occur in one. Therefore, you should often stay in that frame. It is not only the most difficult task for many people, but such people will also hinder others from entering it. Most of the great people of the world not only associate with a very limited group of people but they are also motivated to stay away from certain associations and friendships. Such people have made progress by completely abstaining from imitating the ideas of others. Because they have their methods and measures, it will not be a difficult task to overcome. The opportunities won like this are immense in the world.

Their specialty is that most of the great people who have stepped towards this kind of strength have made tough decisions and did not follow the opinions of others, because it is easy for one to express an idea methodically. Most of them will fail in implementing it. It is a fool's errand to take advice from the failed characters of such a society. Because there is no reason for someone else to use the methods they used and failed again. Therefore, most of the time meaningful and correct advice is given by people who have had good experiences. As you move forward in your journey as a player, it is natural that you will also have a variety of ideas and methods lined up in front of you. So constantly refer to that presence. Whoever holds the strength in different fields, his aims and goals are compatible with the aims and goals of others, but due to the diversity in the field, the methods used to reach strength are not suitable for someone using another subject. For example, the methods used to move forward by an engineer, or a doctor may not be suitable for you as a player. Do not attempt to use or extract such methods.

No one can state that the performance or existence of a player must happen in this way. In any book published in the world, even if it contains the opinion of the author, no one in the world has ever expressed an opinion or a tradition that the reader must follow one hundred percent. It also has no authority to make such a statement. Therefore, in this book also the author is just analyzing how one reaches or acquires a new path in playing. Or just a method followed by that author. The final decision or verdict rests with you.

You are now a step ahead in the field of performing. It must be directed to the measures that can take its growth and another step forward. He has a good understanding of the methods used by any person who has entered a certain powerful plane to reach that plane. Without leaving those methods and advancing them more strongly, will surely strengthen its survival.

Try publishing a mini book out of the content of the workshops you gave on a change in playing. Be sure to launch it as a mini book. Because, unlike the school or university system, the more pages and chapters a subject has on external music, the stronger the book becomes, but it is questionable whether the reader will focus on such a comprehensive analysis in today's busy world. Therefore, make sure to condense only the essentials into a small (limited number of pages and few chapters) book. Briefly analyze only what is necessary.

Attend a concert in a foreign country to achieve strong growth in your career if you participated in concerts or organized such concerts in your native land where you live or were born. For this purpose, there are many people, institutions, and companies who organize various concerts in the world. Having obtained such information on the Internet, you can inform them. Your playlists and videos on the Internet (YouTube) or Spotify, Apple Music, Amazon music, Tidal, Deezer, Pandora etc., will serve you well. Its specialty is that there is a special demand for your creations. The world is constantly interested in inventions and creations which will bring you more benefits. No matter what instrument you play or master, many players have recognized the world of any musical instrument. But the difference in your playing or the advantage you have for modern style, color, rhythm, and shape can be considered important here. Man, always has a desire to get closer to a new taste, a new rhythm, or a new shape.

If you have published a lesson or a series of lessons on the internet (YouTube) on the musical instrument you have mastered on your journey like this, add another lesson or two to that series of lessons today. That newly added lesson or instructional video goes deeper than the previous one and shows more interest in an aspect of the product that has not been seen before or that other instructor has not presented. Especially if it contains things like the rare problems that a person faces in practicing, various new trends to get closer to his musical instrument, what to do and what to remove for his mental improvement, opening a facet of his instrument that he has not seen before, it is the development of your existence that you wish for. It is sure to be confirmed through.

A player who excels in playing the instrument will be invited to workshops and seminars. You should take advantage of those workshops or seminars as your knowledge has increased nowadays. The experience you have developed is powerful for this task. Only such an experienced person can always give successful advice and warnings. In the same way, giving advice and knowledge to others who are not perfect in existence and experience is a great harm. But the stage or situation you are in now is suitable for it and for these workshops and conferences, a new color or shape of playing modern technology as well as how a man approaches new concepts and new thoughts and the methods that bring them closer should be added for your work. In the same way, anyone who has spent a long time with their instrument can use for these situations what is unique to him or what he has recognized and understood from experience that many other players have not seen. If you participate in concerts in a foreign country, you must have your creations on the Internet on YouTube and Spotify, Apple Music, Amazon Music, TikTok etc., because the listener expects it after the concert, it contributes to the popularity of your music in foreign countries through sales. You should have a keen interest in the recordings of those works and the recording should be of international standards and should be able to bring out another strong aspect of your playing.

The cover design for the album must be created by a well-experienced designer because most people are interested in the external appearance and value of the content first. If you are hoping to publish a photograph of yours on the front cover that task must be handed over to a professional photographer. Therefore, it should take a very modern shape and at the same time, the style or theme of your playing should be visible through it, because there is a pattern or shape that shows certain fields, so your pattern should be in that image, and you should also be interested in the combination of colors.

Above all, you should be interested in the techniques used for your fresh creations. The player excels in composition based on his technical prowess. Using the same techniques in the same style for every composition does not add variety or freshness. So, the extended techniques you use should include some slightly different rhythms and different tones. Then the listener will be able to experience a different flavor and a new shape, and your progress will be encouraged.

When looking at some creations in the music industry, it will be clear that modern music is different. There is a famous saying that 'How playing one note expressively is better than playing a hundred notes.' Anyway, whatever you play or compose there must be something pleasing, a message which contain a meaningful idea or which is able to convey a solution for the listener. Along with the changes in the modern world, there is a need for new waves in music, but the changes that occur in crossing certain limits are dangerous. Music, including art, strongly influences human hearts and changes human attitudes and thoughts. It is right to describe music as a great therapy for humans for some of their problems and issues or as an art that has the power to heal some mental problems. The facts are that when modern music's shape or message surpasses the function of healing the human soul, it is dangerous to build violent and distorted concepts in the youth. It is harmful to the world. Although the social representation of a robot is very subtle, it is a good investment in the coming world population decline. With the prediction that the world's population will decrease rapidly by the year 2100, it is a smart move to create such designs in the world. This is a good investment for the future shortage of human labor. But it is very dangerous for man's thoughts and thinking to change in ways that are not compatible with human existence. No one can make a legal system or prohibit such things for such changes in music. Art is for the people. Likewise, it is for the betterment of the people. So, in any piece of music, it will be meaningless if the necessary message that the listener is looking for is not contained in the piece. Likewise, it is dangerous for a message that does not fit society or a confusing message to enter the human mind through it. Society must move forward in some correct pattern. If there is any adverse change in it, the social explorers will also find their way unclear and will have to put in a lot of effort to correct it. A country needs intelligent, disciplined, sensitive, and efficient people. The absence of such a generation will certainly not lead to the betterment of the country but will be a country that has followed the wrong path. No matter how powerful a country is economically, various changes in human concepts will strongly affect its survival.

Due to the current global economic downturn (especially due to the 2019 Covid pandemic and the 2022 February war between Russia and Ukraine), many of the world's scheduled music concerts have been canceled and some have been postponed. Due to the high cost of airline tickets, the high cost of other transportation, the high cost of advertising, as well as the economic recession in Europe, concert ticket sales have slowed down and decreased. But anyway, there won't be a world without music. From the primitive age [well established in the Middle Era] music had a strong link with mankind.

It is important for anyone who loves western music to turn to or listen to the works of modern composers who are now imitating the composers such as Bach or Beethoven. It is correct to characterize modern classical music as a meaningful and profound experiment in form and sound. Although the era of classical music was in Europe (1750 - 1820), today it has spread all over the world. This has been revealed by the world's leading newspapers, music magazines, and symphonies. In many musical styles Pop, Rock, Latin, Country and Metal [to name a few] genres there are differences or new waves today. Some of the powerful composers living today (for classical music) are mentioned, and their powerful creations are also mentioned below. By listening to these you will be able to understand its diversity.

1. Kaija Saariaho (b-1952) Petals
2. Arvo Part (b-1935) Fratres
3. Jennifer Higdon (b-1962) Blue Cathedral
4. Steve Reich (86 Years) Piece of Wood
5. Unsuk Chin (b-1961) Subito con Forza
6. Hildur Gudnadottir (b-1982) Erupting Light
7. Mason Bates (b - 1977) Mothership
8. Anna Clyne (b-1980) Mythologies

Modern composers are interested in the rhythm of the music, bringing the instrument to the fore, the tone color, its shape, form, and extended techniques, it's an important event nowadays to give priority to the rhythm and to show more interest in the variation in the playing of the musical instrument. Melody and Harmony no longer exist in most modern compositions today.

If you research any musical instrument amidst these transformations, they also undergo certain setbacks with time and due to various traditions (Genres). Another instrument or another tradition emerges instead of that neglected instrument. The main reason for this decline is the difficulty of maintaining a certain tradition or musical instrument in a monotonous manner for a long time. Players have taken their instruments as far as they could go, which is the other reason for this. Any change in its impact or presentation will inevitably lead to popularity and stability in society.

In the same way, after the players have gathered many fans and are popular with the use of a certain musical instrument, a group of players who have picked up that musical instrument should gradually enter the field. The absence of a back row for those players who were considered heroes from the beginning also causes the popularity of the instrument to decrease.

Organizations for the survival of the world's music should do more than join the industry for the sake of profit. In an era where many talented young and old energetic people are lined up to win the music industry, their modern procedure should be more meaningful and different than before. The concepts of bringing the generation forward should also be exposed by them. That service will directly affect the process of maintaining the field. One of them is that music is the most popular subject in the world. There are many unseen and unheard aspects of the music field. It has no age limit, high or low, educated or illiterate, or rural or urban. Since there is no urban connection, more new organizations should join this and organizations that can identify aspects that are unseen and unheard more than before. Traffic congestion is a process built for the needs of people. In many countries, rapid measures have been launched for this purpose, but those measures are not by vehicle manufacturing companies in those countries, through the governments of those countries.

For the competition and congestion of the music industry there are some organizations today, but more organizations should be created, and it should happen as a service and advancement in the field, otherwise, the music industry will be lost to a very talented group of people who are looking to enter the industry, and the emergence of new concepts and new waves will also slowdown in various other fields. Parallel to the progress and development, if such changes do not happen in the music industry, the decline of the industry has been shown in this book. There must be leaders in the industry. The fans have inevitably become very close to their styles and there must be a change with time. For that change, the new generation is a good investment. In 2008 – 2009, many economic specialists and researchers did not notice the severe economic decline that occurred in the world. Likewise, the music industry will continue to progress for many years until 2023. Some setbacks may occur along the way. There must be a preparation for that. Due to the 2020-2021 Covid 19 pandemic, despite the music industry downturn, 2022 has seen rapid growth in popularity and fan attendance at major concerts and festivals around the world has doubled and tripled.

In the same way, in 2020, the sales of some musical instruments [the guitar] grew in a record way, and the representation of women in it was more than before. The sales of the acoustic guitar surpassed all types of guitars, and the income of some organizations that suffered losses from the sale of guitars has been confirmed by the reports.

Whether it is a woman or a man, no matter what age they are, their external shape can be adjusted to extremely different changes. It doesn't happen by chance and for that, different clothes, hairstyles, shoes, walking style, face shape (can be changed by different colors), speaking style and many other things should be used for this purpose. The result is that the expected person becomes visible through these changes. Similarly, your playing can present various shapes, colors, rhythms, and messages using different techniques. But for that, as said before, you must approach various successful new methods.

Look back from where you are now. It is a meaningful long

journey full of memories. You are not affected at all. Any fatigue will be eclipsed by intense pleasure and happiness. You have stepped in the direction you sought, and you are at its gate. Open it. What you see is a fertile field. It is the field you have sown. It is built for your survival. Go a step further and enjoy it. Take a few more steps forward. Its other doors are closed. It's time to open it up. Once it is opened, there are many more doors to open. All of them must be opened by the players of the world. That is your role. Why? It is in the name of the progress of the performance. Are you not yet ready to use the appropriate methods for it? This is your time. Now is the right time. You have to Join with those musicians. Many musicians will gradually step into that world. It should happen for the progress of the player and the performance.

ABOUT THE AUTHOR

Amaranath Ranatunga

is a Guitarist and Composer. He uses his own extended techniques in his compositions to create a new wave in music. At present, he is lecturing guitar as a visiting lecturer at the University of Kelaniya, Sri Lanka for BA and MA degree programs in music. The three CDs he published and another two albums ['Your Way' and 'The Impact'] are available on streaming platforms. "New Wave for a Musician" is his third book and in this book, he tries to convey the value of a new genre for a player who is playing any musical instrument.

1."He is Fantastic and a wonderful guitarist".
The EntreMusicians, USA

2."His proficiency and competence in Western music is an asset to

Sri Lanka as well as to the international community".
SBS Radio Cooperation, Australia

3."Amarnath Ranatunga's students display solid technique and advanced musical skills. I am highly impressed with the tremendous work he is doing for the performance and education of the classical guitar in Sri Lanka."
Dr. Paul Cesarczyk Guitar Department Chair, Mahidol University College of Music, Thailand

4."He is one of the most respected Guitarists and Music educationists in his country and travels widely giving concerts and lectures".
Indian Guitar Federation of India

BOOKS BY THIS AUTHOR

Classical And Flamenco Guitar

First Print: 2007 (with CD)
Second Print: 2015 (New Edition)

Dawning Of An Instrumentalists

First Print: 2014

www.ingramcontent.com/pod-product-compliance
Lightning Source LLC
LaVergne TN
LVHW091100150826
845673LV00002B/663

* 9 7 8 6 2 4 9 4 7 3 7 0 6 *